Out Of Focus

Out Of Focus

Vincent Phoenix Sumah

CONTENTS

INTRODUCTION

B reaking news: we live in a society built by and for the most "average" human. In North America, that means a white, cisgender, straight, neurotypical Christian man. (Yes, even though there are statistically more women than men, we live in a patriarchal world, so men are still seen as the default human being.)

The truth is, the further you stray from that "default," the more likely you are to face disadvantages as you move through life.

For many, school years are a particularly tough time. And I don't just mean struggling with academics. Schools (their structures, rules, teachers, and students) form tiny micro-societies that reflect larger societal systems. As a neurodivergent therapist who works with young neurodivergent adults, I see firsthand how these systems shape human development.

Spoiler alert: the impact isn't always positive.

Oh, and I've lived it, too. I wasn't just a neurodivergent student; I was one for almost 20 years of my life.

I wrote this book to help people with different executive functions better navigate the challenges of learning and survive (or even thrive!) in the micro-societies of schools. My hope is to reduce the risk and intensity of potential trauma, because the scars school leaves can last a lifetime.

Here's what you'll find in this book:

- Short paragraphs, so you can tackle just one at a time without overwhelm.
- **So**me **sections writt**en in **bio**nic **rea**ding **for**mat to **ma**ke **th**em **ea**sier to **fol**low.
- A TL;DR (too long, didn't read) summary after every key point or idea.

- If you skip to the last section, you'll find all the TL;DRs in one place, so you can get a quick overview of what the book covers.

One important note: when we talk about ADHDers and autistic people in this book, we're speaking in general terms. Every individual is unique, with their own traits and struggles. The goal here is to give you a broad understanding of these neurotypes, not to generalize or over-simplify. And if you see the term "ADHDer" used here, know that it's a name commonly embraced by the ADHD community and is meant with respect.

I hope this book feels like a companion on your journey. ENJOY!

THE BEAUTY OF
NEURODIVERSITY

First, what is neurodiversity?

The term "neurodiversity" was first used in September 1998 by a neurodiversity advocate, Harvey Blume, in an article for The Atlantic called "Neurodiversity, On the neurological underpinnings of Geekdom".

> *"Neurodiversity may be every bit as crucial for the human race as biodiversity is for life in general. Who can say what form of wiring will prove best at any given moment? Cybernetics and computer culture, for example, may favor a somewhat autistic cast of mind. That would lend neurological significance to Jon Katz's foregrounding of Geek Force. And it would make ISNT's argument for neurodiversity not only timely but quite possibly irresistible."* (Blume, 1998)

Neurodiversity **des**cribes the **inc**redible **r**ange of **wa**ys **hu**man **br**ains **ca**n be **wi**red. Unlike what many neurotypical people (or as I like to call them, "the workers"—more on that later) might assume, there's no single "normal" way for a brain to develop or function. Even though all human brains share the same evolutionary "base" as animals, the wiring varies from person to person. And just like any other kind of human difference, every neurotype[1] deserves the same rights, respect, and opportunities, whether from society, governments, or institutions.

But, **as** with other **forms** of **dis**crimination, **soc**iety has **cre**ated **cat**egories to **div**ide us. On one **side**, we have **"neu**rotypicals," the **group** of **bra**ins that **soc**iety has **dec**ided are the **"def**ault."

On the other **side**, there's **every**one else: **those** of us who **fall** under the **broad umb**rella **term** **"neu**rodivergent."

Neurodivergence includes a variety of brains that process and experience the world differently, whether through how we think, sense, connect with others, or reflect. This term covers inborn conditions like autism, ADHD, dyslexia, and Tourette's Syndrome, among others. Some people believe it should also include disorders like OCD, BPD (Borderline Personality Disorder), or Bipolar Disorder, since these conditions also involve unique ways of perceiving and interacting with the world. At the end of the day, the definition of neurodivergence depends on where you choose to draw the line between what's considered a "typical" brain and what's considered different.

---

[1] A type of brain, in terms of how a person interprets and responds to social cues, etc. (wiktionary.org, 2023)

TL;DR : Neurodiversity depicts the vast range of diversity and differences in how the human brain is wired. It is often divided between neurotypicals and "all the others" (neurodivergents).

The brain, this ruler

What makes a human (or any other animal, for that matter) **experience the world**, **behave** in any situation, or **enjoy (or not enjoy!) life**? **That's the brain.**

I feel we don't give the brain enough credit for its role in how we **perceive and process everything** around us. The brain is where everything (and I mean **everything**) we experience gets processed. And it does this in its own unique way, based on the **neural connections** it creates throughout our lives.

The brain has **one primary job**: to ensure we survive, both as individuals and as a species. Most of the things it records, and that later turn into our **behaviors** and **habits**, are either:

1. Certified by the brain as **safe** or
2. A **defense mechanism** to protect us from perceived threats.

The two main "things" that **subconsciously** create new neural connections (yes, there's also a way to consciously change them, we'll get to that later) are:

1. **The eight senses** (yes, eight, you read that right!)
2. **The vast range of emotions and feelings.**

Through these experiences, the brain determines if something is:

- **Safe or unsafe**
- **Good or bad**
- **Logical or nonsensical**

Based on this processing, the brain creates **connections** for the future.

However, these connections aren't always accurate. Sometimes, the brain creates **biased shortcuts** : it might link two unrelated events and believe one causes the other, even if that's not true.

Every brain forms different links because each of us is born with a **unique set of personality traits,** and we all have **different life experiences** that shape those connections. But under all these unique links and patterns, what we call the "**typical brain**" has the same basic **executive functions** and processes.

It's like working on a **Mac** and a **PC.**
Both are computers that let you browse the internet, play games, and use software. But the **user interface (UI)** is different. The **features** and **settings** are different. Some games and software are simply not available on a Mac, and others are not available on a PC.

Still, both computers are **programmed to achieve similar goals**, with a few exceptions. The differences lie mostly in the **processes** (the keys, software, and features you use to get what you want done). We all accept that.

Now... what if we use this computer analogy to explain the differences between **neurotypical (NT)** and **neurodivergent (ND)** brains?

Let's say that **ADHD** and **autism** executive functions are like a Mac, while neurotypical executive functions are like a PC.

For example: **PC users** are used to doing right-clicks for many tasks. It's a standard part of how the system works.
But **there are no right-clicks on a Mac.** You can fight with your mouse as much as you want, but it won't work. Instead, you need to use **Control+Click** to perform the same function.

Here's another example: you **cannot install iMovie** on a PC. iMovie is a video-editing software built by and for Apple products. You can try as much as you want to install it on a PC, but it won't work. **The codes are not compatible.**

To keep this analogy going:
A **neurodivergent (ND) brain** is like a Mac, while a **neurotypical (NT) brain** is like a PC. The **base codes** of these systems are fundamentally different. This means that some "features" in NT brains **cannot be accurately replicated** in ND brains, even by "trying harder" (and vice versa).

If the feature doesn't exist in a brain's operating system, you can make all the effort in the world, but it won't magically appear. **You have to find a workaround.** The result might not look exactly like what you intended, **but it could end up being even better.**

A different **base code** leads to different kinds of **neural connections**. These connections influence how we:

- **Experience life** through our senses and emotions,
- **Shape our reality,**
- **Behave, and**
- **Understand the world.**

And here's the thing: most of this, just like in NT brains, is completely **subconscious**, **automatic**, and **involuntary**.

TL;DR : The brain rules everything we experience, and neurotypical (NT) brains have a different "base code" than neurodivergent (ND) brains, impacting the way all the other connections are created.

Okay, now what?

Now that we've established that **neurotypical (NT) brains** are not only different from **neurodivergent (ND) brains** in **neuron connections**, but also in their **base code**, we can see why many things in society, designed with NT brains in mind, don't always work for ND individuals.

But what are these "things" in society that **assume everyone's brain works the same way?**

1. Social Norms and Unwritten Rules

These are the invisible guidelines that dictate how people **connect with others**, what is considered "acceptable" behavior, and how we use **figurative expressions** like metaphors or sarcasm.

2. The Concept of "Functioning"

Society assumes there is a standard way to "function" that includes:

- **Daily tasks** like cleaning, eating, and sleeping,
- **Family roles** and social expectations,
- The assumption that these things come naturally or easily to everyone.

3. The Work System

Modern work life is rooted in a **capitalist model**, which includes:

- **9-to-5 schedules**, 5 days a week,
- **Hierarchical systems** where you're judged by your productivity,
- The belief that your job **defines your identity.**
  This system works for many NTs, but it can feel like an impossible maze for NDs.

4. The School System

The school system is built to **prepare people for work**, and since it mimics the work system, it also assumes NT brains as the default. Classrooms often reward behaviors like sitting still, focusing for long periods, and following instructions without question, all tasks that can be especially challenging for ND students.

These four areas (**social norms, functioning, work, and school**) shape nearly every aspect of a person's life. **If these systems don't work for you, it's not because you're "wrong."** It's because they were built for a brain type that may not match your own.

What This Book Will Focus On

While we won't dive deeply into **social norms** or **functioning** in this book (those are topics we'll save for a book about autism), we will focus on **the school and work systems.**

Why?

- These systems rely heavily on NT executive functions, like planning, organization, and multitasking.
- They are also **major sources of frustration, confusion, and suffering** for people with different executive functions.

By understanding how these systems operate and why they feel so challenging, we hope to give neurodivergent people both **relief** and **hope**:

Relief

To learn that there is **nothing wrong with you** and everything wrong with a society that doesn't accommodate neurodivergent brains.

Hope

To believe that it is possible to build an **enriching life** and even **reshape society** despite neurotypical constraints.

This book isn't about fixing yourself. It's about understanding the systems around you and finding ways to thrive, just as you are.

TL;DR : Trying to reach neurotypical expectations of life (and they are everywhere) when you are neurodivergent often leads to suffering, confusion, and frustration. There is nothing wrong with ND brains, and society needs to be more inclusive.

2

EXECUTIVE FUNCTIONS

As we mentioned earlier, the entire **school and work system** is built on the assumption that everyone's **executive functions (EFs)** work the same way.

But what exactly are **executive functions**, and why are they so important?

Let's jump into it!

What Are Executive Functions (EFs)?

Executive functions (EFs) are a set of **brain processes** that help us **plan, organize, and accomplish tasks.** Without them, many everyday activities would feel chaotic or impossible to complete.

These processes are controlled by the **frontal lobe**—the part of your brain located, you guessed it, **right behind your forehead.**

Think of EFs as your brain's **"management system"**: they help you decide what needs to be done, how to do it, and when to start.

Why Are EFs So Important?

EFs are called into action whenever we need to:

- **Start tasks** (like writing an email or cleaning your room).
- **Plan and organize** (like deciding the steps needed to prepare dinner).

- **Stay focused** (like concentrating during a meeting or study session).
- **Manage emotions** (like staying calm when things don't go as planned).
- **Adapt to change** (like adjusting to a last-minute schedule shift).

In short, EFs are the tools we use to **navigate life's challenges**, whether it's acing a test, handling work deadlines, or simply getting out of bed on time.

NT vs. ND Executive Functions

Here's the tricky part: the **school and work system** assumes everyone's **executive functions** work in the same **neurotypical (NT)** way. This means they're designed for people who:

- Can **start tasks easily** without procrastination or overwhelm.
- **Follow multi-step** instructions smoothly.
- **Stay organized and manage** their time effectively.
- **Regulate emotions** during stress.

But for many **neurodivergent (ND)** people, executive functions often **don't work the same way.** ADHD brains process tasks **differently**, with unique strengths and challenges. The problem isn't the brain—it's that **the systems** refuse to adapt.

Important Note

Before we dive deeper into executive functions, here's something important to remember:

Every neurodivergent person is different.

While ND people may share similar experiences with executive functions, not everyone will have the **same strengths or limitations.** What's more, **EFs can change over time** based on factors like:

- Stress levels,
- Life circumstances, or
- Environment.

The information in this book will give you a broad overview of how EFs work in ADHD brains, but it won't represent everyone's exact experience.

TL;DR: **Executive functions (EFs)** are brain processes controlled by the **frontal lobe** that help us **plan, start, and complete tasks.**

School and work systems assume everyone's EFs function the same way, but **this isn't true.**

EFs vary widely, especially between **neurotypical (NT)** and **neurodivergent (ND)** people.

Each ND person experiences EFs **differently**, and these strengths and challenges can even **change over time.**

Deductive Reasoning

Deductive reasoning is the ability to **figure out precisely what's expected** in a task from vague instructions.

For example:

- **"Clean your room."**
- **"Order the materials."**
- **"Make more effort."**
- **"Write the assessment."**

For someone whose **deductive reasoning comes naturally**, their brain automatically **fills in the blanks** with what makes the most sense. They don't need extra details because their brain connects the dots **subconsciously** and they can jump right into action.

How ADHD Brains Experience Deductive Reasoning

For most people with ADHD, deductive reasoning **doesn't come automatically**. Most **ADHDers** and **autistic individuals** can't "invent a way to fill in the blanks" if they haven't been through a **similar situation before.**

Take **"clean your room"** as an example:

- If nobody has ever told them specifically **what that task includes** (e.g., "pick up dirty clothes and put them in the laundry, sweep the floor, make your bed"), it's not precise enough.
- They might feel stuck or overwhelmed, unsure where to **start or what is expected**.

It's not a **lack of intelligence** or a skill they simply need to "learn." Instead, their brain **requires more information upfront** to perform the task.

Why This Happens

The truth is, **neurodivergent brains and neurotypical brains process instructions differently.**

- For **NT people**, their brains naturally fill in the blanks. They might not even realize they're doing this because it's **subconscious and automatic**.
- For **most ADHD people**, the brain doesn't automatically fill the blanks unless they've encountered a **similar task or situation in the past.**

This difference isn't something either group can control. Just as **NT brains** can't stop themselves from filling in the blanks, **ADHD and Autistic brains** can't stop themselves from **needing more clarity.**

What ADHD People Need for New Tasks

When ADHD/autistic people face a **new or unfamiliar task**, they may need:

1. A clear, **step-by-step list** of what's expected (preferably written).
2. Details about steps that might seem "obvious" to NT brains.

For example, instead of saying:

- **"Clean your room,"** try something like:
  1. **Pick up dirty clothes and put them in the laundry basket.**
  2. **Make your bed.**
  3. **Sweep the floor.**
  4. **Put books back on the shelf.**

This approach reduces confusion, **eliminates guesswork**, and helps ND people feel more confident and capable.

What It's Not

This difference in deductive reasoning is **not**:

- A lack of intelligence.
- A skill that someone can "just learn" without the right kind of support.

It's simply a different way of processing tasks—and it's just as valid.

TL;DR

- **Deductive reasoning** is the ability to **fill in the blanks** when information is missing.
- Neurotypical (NT) brains do this subconsciously, while autistic and ADHD brains often **require clear instructions** to know what's expected.
- For autistic and ADHD people, tasks require **detailed, step-by-step instructions,** especially when the task is new or unfamiliar.

Planning and prioritization

Planning and prioritization are brain functions that help us figure out:

1. **What to start with in a task,** and
2. **In what order to tackle the steps.**

It's the skill that allows us to **envision the future** and mentally plan out the best way to accomplish a goal. It's about anticipating what's ahead and preparing for it.

How NT Brains Handle Planning and Prioritization

For someone with **typical executive functions (EFs)**:

- Their brain automatically creates a **mental roadmap** for tasks.
- They can **roughly envision the steps** they need to take, what to do first, and how to proceed.
- Once this plan is clear, they can just **follow it to the finish line.**

This ability to **plan ahead** is closely tied to other EF skills, like **time perception** (being able to estimate how long tasks will take). It's like having a built-in GPS: NT brains map out the route and then drive straight toward their destination.

How many ND Brains Handle Planning and Prioritization

For **ADHDers** and **autistic people**, the process is **different**:

- **The mental plan doesn't happen automatically.**
- Instead, we need to **manually and consciously create the plan** step by step.

This takes both **energy** and **time**, and it can feel overwhelming, especially if we're also struggling with **deductive reasoning** (the ability to identify the steps in the first place).

- The more we do something, the better we become at knowing the steps. Repetition and familiarity help.
- **But even with practice, the process never becomes automatic.** It always requires effort.

The Challenge of Prioritization in ND Brains

Another difference for ADHD and some autistic people is how we approach **prioritization.**

For NT brains:

- Tasks are naturally ranked by importance.

For ADHD brains:

- **Everything feels equally important.**
- The result? It's hard to know **what to focus on first**—or if we're focusing on the "right" thing at all.

This lack of prioritization can leave us feeling stuck or paralyzed, especially when faced with a long to-do list or competing demands.

The Energy Cost of Planning for ADHD Brains

Because planning and prioritization require conscious effort, ADHDers:

- Often experience **mental fatigue** or burnout when creating task plans.
- May struggle to get started if the steps or priorities aren't clear enough.

It's not laziness or lack of intelligence. Our brains just need **more input** and **more time** to create a plan.

TL;DR:

- **Planning and prioritization** involve creating a mental **roadmap** for tasks and ranking them by importance.
- NT brains do this automatically, while **ND brains must do it manually** through conscious effort.
- For ND people, planning takes time, energy, and familiarity—and prioritization can be especially tricky because **everything feels equally important.**

Organization

Organization is the brain function that helps us arrange our environment and bring **order and structure** to the items and activities in our lives.

It's what allows us to:

- **Clean up** and put things back where they belong after an activity.
- Keep our **workspace or room** neat and in order.
- Think about what we'll need for the day and **bring it all** with us.
- Protect important things like **school supplies** or documents by not tossing them randomly into our bag.

How Organization Supports Our Daily Lives

Organization works hand in hand with other executive functions, like **time perception** (which we'll explore further on). Together, they help us:

- **Get ready** and leave on time.
- **Arrive where we need to be** without feeling rushed or unprepared.

But it's not just about keeping our physical surroundings tidy. **Organization also applies to our thoughts and communication.**

For example:

- When we explain something, **organized thinking** helps us create a beginning, middle, and end to the story.
- Without proper organization, our thoughts may feel **scattered,** making it harder for others to follow what we're saying, or for us to follow our own train of thought.

How Organization Works in ND Brains

For **ADHDers** and **autistic people**, organizing our surroundings and thoughts isn't automatic. Instead, we have to:

1. **Manually and consciously organize** every time it's needed.
2. Use a lot of **energy and focus** (and this can add up quickly when it's required constantly throughout the day).

When life adds extra layers, like **stress** or **fatigue**, it becomes even harder to keep things organized. Here's what might happen:

- **Physical spaces:** Our bedroom or desk may become **more chaotic than usual.**
- **Daily essentials:** We might leave the house and **forget important things,** like lunch, schoolwork, or supplies.
- **Thoughts:** Our mind feels even more **scattered** than normal, making it **hard to communicate** or complete tasks.

TL;DR:

- **Organization** is the ability to **bring order to our environment** and thoughts.
- It helps us **keep spaces tidy,** remember what we need, and **communicate clearly.**
- ND brains **don't organize automatically**. This requires **time, energy, and focus,** which can be hard to manage under stress or fatigue.

Problem Solving

Problem solving is the ability to **adapt rapidly** to an unexpected situation or obstacle and **find a solution.**

The brain, more or less automatically:

1. **Parses through past experiences and learned strategies.**
2. **Breaks the problem into smaller parts**, making it easier to solve.

This skill helps us figure out how to reach a goal, adjust as we go, and learn from missteps by developing new strategies. Whether it's a work issue, a family matter, or a social challenge, problem solving allows us to adapt and move forward.

How Problem Solving Works in NT Brains

For most NT individuals, problem solving happens **automatically and instinctively.**

- Their brain draws from past experiences, **suggesting solutions** without much conscious effort.
- They instinctively **break the problem into manageable steps** or adjust their approach when things don't work out.

It's like having a **mental GPS** that recalculates the route to a goal when obstacles appear.

How Problem Solving Works in ND Brains

For **ADHDers** and **autistic individuals**, problem solving often works **differently.**

When faced with an unexpected obstacle:

- **The mind may go blank**, making it hard to come up with a solution on the spot.
- Or, **too many thoughts** might arrive all at once, creating overwhelm instead of clarity.

Unlike NT brains, ND individuals can't always instinctively think of alternatives. For them, problem solving:

- Requires **conscious effort** and **manual processing** of the situation.
- Demands **time** and **energy** that might not be available in stressful or overwhelming moments.

How ND Brains Can Build Problem-Solving Skills

Problem-solving is a skill that can be **acquired and strengthened**, but it often requires **support** and **positive experiences** to develop.

Here's how ND individuals can improve problem-solving:

- **Safe and positive experiences:** The more they encounter problems in a supportive environment, the less likely they'll freeze when new challenges arise.
- **Step-by-step learning:** Facing challenges gradually, with encouragement, helps build confidence and reduces overwhelm.

The first step in building problem-solving skills is **reducing the freeze response**, making it easier to engage with challenges over time.

Why Problem Solving Is an Everyday Challenge

You may have noticed that problem solving is deeply connected to other executive functions, like **planning, prioritization, and organization.** They're all part of the same **mental toolkit**, and they rely on the same part of the brain.

For ND individuals, **executive functions aren't naturally designed for this kind of work**, so solving problems, meeting expectations, and managing daily challenges is an **ongoing struggle.**

Add tiredness, stress, or burnout into the mix, and these challenges grow exponentially. That's why ADHDers and autistic people often need **support before they reach a breaking point** where their ability to function becomes compromised.

TL;DR:
- **Problem solving** is the ability to adapt to unexpected challenges by **parsing past experiences** or **breaking problems into smaller parts.**
- NT brains handle this **instinctively**, while ND brains must do it **manually**, which takes **time, energy,** and conscious effort.
- ND individuals can build problem-solving skills by having **positive, supportive experiences** with obstacles over time.
- Problem solving is linked to **planning, prioritization, and organization**, making it an everyday challenge for ND people.

Working Memory

Working memory, also known as **short-term memory**, is the brain's ability to temporarily store and manage information we need in the moment.

It's what allows us to:

- Remember the **name of someone you just met**.
- Keep track of the **tasks you need to do**.
- Recall **what you were just saying or doing**.
- Know where you put your **cell phone, keys, or book** (so you can grab them again soon).

How Working Memory Differs in ND Brains

For **NT brains**, working memory might feel like having **20 slots** to temporarily store information.

For **ADHDers** and many **autistic individuals**, it's more like having **3 slots.** At least, that's how I like to picture it.

- If more than 3 pieces of information need to be stored, the brain has to **make space** by discarding one of the already stored items.
- This is why ADHDers and autistic people are often seen as **forgetful**: their brain simply doesn't have enough **storage slots** for everything.

Why Forgetting Happens

It's important to remember (no pun intended!) that **forgetting isn't about importance or effort.**

- It's not that ND people don't **care** about what they're trying to remember.

- Their brain simply doesn't have enough **working memory slots** and will **delete information automatically**, without permission.

Sometimes, the brain doesn't even **record information at all.** For example:

- You can't "forget" or "remember" where you put your **cell phone or keys** if your brain **never stored that information in the first place.**
- This can happens when the brain is overwhelmed or distracted, and the detail (like where you placed an item) was never registered in working memory.

Why This Matters

The everyday life of anyone in modern society is packed with **short-term information** to remember. For ADHDers and some autistic people, this constant demand on working memory can feel like an uphill battle. **The brain does its best**, but it's limited by its design.

Forgetfulness is not a reflection of **laziness** or **carelessness**. It's a result of how ND brains process and store short-term information differently from NT brains.

TL;DR:

- **Working memory** (short-term memory) is the brain's ability to temporarily store information we need in the moment.
- **ADHDers** and many **autistic people** have **fewer memory slots** than NT brains, so they can't store as much short-term information.
- Forgetting happens when the brain **runs out of space** or **never records the information to begin with.**

Attention

An **ADHD brain** is never quiet. There are always **multiple thoughts** and **ideas swirling** around at the same time.

From the outside, it might look like ADHDers **can't focus** or **pay attention**, but the truth is more complex. Here's why attention can be so difficult:

The Constant Noise in an ADHD Brain

Think of a time when you tried to **read a book** while people were talking loudly next to you. It was probably hard to focus, right?

Now imagine that this is what happens **constantly** in an ADHD brain. It's not like loud shouting, but it's like trying to read or watch a movie while **three people are talking over each other** right next to you.

This constant background "noise" in their mind makes focusing on one thing at a time incredibly **distracting and exhausting.**

How Focus is Tied to Interest and Dopamine

For ADHDers and many autistic individuals, **focus isn't about effort**. It's about **interest.**

Here's why:

- The ADHD brain produces **dopamine** (the "feel-good" brain chemical) based on how interesting or stimulating something is.
- The more **dopamine** a task produces, the easier it is for the ADHD brain to **shut out distractions** and focus.

This means:

- If a task is boring or unengaging, the ADHD brain will struggle to stay focused, no matter how hard the person "tries."

- But if a task is **highly interesting** or **stimulating**, the ADHD brain can enter **hyperfocus**, which is a state where they're fully absorbed in the activity for hours, days, or even weeks.

The Power of Intrinsic Motivation

ADHD and autistic brains are built on **intrinsic motivation.**

- They can **dive deep** into topics that interest them and learn a new skill or master a subject in record time.
- This hyperfocus is an **incredible strength**, but society often fails to value or encourage it.

Why "Making More Effort" Doesn't Work

ADHD is not a brain with an **"attention deficit."** Instead, it's a brain that **cannot focus for long** on something that doesn't provide enough **dopamine** or **stimulation.**

Forcing an ADHDer or autistic person to keep going when their brain has **"had enough"** is:

1. **Useless:** The brain will stop processing information, no matter how much effort they put in.
2. **Exhausting:** Their **energy drops rapidly**, and trying to push through will only cause frustration and burnout.

What ADHD and Autistic Brains Need

When their brain **stops cooperating**, ADHDers and autistic people need:

- **A break** to rest or recharge.
- To do something that's **stimulating or interesting** to reset their focus.

This doesn't mean they're lazy! It means their brain is functioning exactly how it's wired to work.

ADHDers and autistic people need to be:

- **Understood** and respected.
- **Never diminished** or called lazy for how their attention works.

TL;DR:
- ADHD and autistic brains give their attention to the **most stimulating and interesting thing** around.
- Forcing them to persist in a boring or unengaging task is **useless and draining.**
- They need **breaks** and time to recharge their attention through activities that bring **dopamine and stimulation.**

Distraction

What's the first thing we tell students?

"You need a clean desk, free of distractions, to focus on studying or homework."

This advice is especially common for **ADHDers**, given their reputation for being "easily distracted." And while this might help some people, it's often **not helpful** for many ADHDers and autistic people.

Here's why:

Their brains struggle to focus in understimulating environments.

Why ADHD and Autistic Brains Need Stimulation

To focus, many ADHDers and autistic people need **just the right level of stimulation**. For example:

- Some may listen to **music** or a podcast.
- Others might **fidget** with something in their hands.
- Some might even have a TV show on in the background.
- A few might juggle **three or four different tasks** at once, jumping between them as they chase dopamine.

"But They Can't Be 100% Efficient That Way!"

You might think, "They can't be 100% efficient if they're distracted!" And you'd probably be right—at least if you're comparing them to **neurotypical standards of efficiency.**

But let's put it into perspective:

- If they're **50% efficient** while multitasking or fidgeting, that might sound like a drop.
- But if you compare it to the **20% efficiency** they'd have in a dull, distraction-free environment... 50% suddenly sounds a lot better, doesn't it?

"How Can They Get to 100% Efficiency?"

Good question—but the answer depends on how you define **"100% efficiency."**

- Is it based on **your standards** of how you think they should perform?
- Or is it based on the rare **times they hyperfocused**, which might not be repeatable under normal circumstances?

Stick around—we'll dive deeper into this in further in the book!

What You Should Know About ADHD and some Autistic Distraction

Here's the truth: ADHD and some autistic brains aren't **"easily distracted."** Their brains are **designed** to:

- Notice every **sound, thought**, and **change in the environment.**
- Stay curious and **explore multiple ideas at once.**

For ADHDers and autistic people, focusing on one thing for hours isn't natural unless it's highly interesting or stimulating.

It takes an incredible amount of **self-discipline** to bring their focus back to a boring task and this kind of self-discipline is rarely taught in a way that works for their brains.

So, instead of forcing them to fight against their nature, we need to understand and respect how their brains work and create environments where they can thrive.

TL;DR:
- The ADHD brain is **designed to notice everything**—sounds, thoughts, and changes in the environment.
- Focusing for hours on a boring task is **not natural** for them.

- They need tasks to be **highly interesting or stimulating** to shut out "distractions" and stay focused.

Time Perception

ADHDers and some **autistic people** don't perceive time the same way as neurotypicals, and they **can't control it**—it's an **inner process.**
Here's the challenge:

- The further away something is in the future, the **blurrier** it becomes to the mind.
- A paper due in **two weeks** feels vague and intangible. **Two weeks or three months? It's all the same.**

Why Deadlines Feel Unreal Until the Last Minute

For ADHDers and some autistic people, deadlines only become **real and tangible** a few days, or sometimes just **a few hours**, before they're due.

Here's how it typically plays out:

1. **"I still have time."** In the early stages, they feel no sense of urgency to start the task.
2. **"Oh no, it's due tomorrow!"** Suddenly, the deadline is close enough to feel real, and they panic (for good reason).
3. They rush to finish the task, often in a last-minute scramble to beat the clock.

This cycle of procrastination isn't about laziness. It's about how their brains process time.

The Pirate Ship Analogy

Imagine standing by the sea, looking at the horizon. You're not wearing your **glasses**, but your friend, who has 20/20 vision, is next to you.

- Your friend spots a **pirate ship** in the distance and warns you to **run and hide.**
- But without your glasses, the ship looks blurry, so you don't feel the same urgency they do.

As the ship gets closer, you can start to see **something**, but you still don't know what it is. It could be a merchant ship, for all you know. Your friend insists it's a pirate ship, and you believe them, but it still doesn't feel **real** to you.

Finally, when the pirate flag becomes clear, you realize the danger. Sometimes you see it **early enough to react** and run, but other times, it's **too late** to escape.

This is what time perception is like for ADHDers and autistic people. Future deadlines are blurry until they're close enough to feel tangible—sometimes **too close.**

Motivation and Time Perception

Time perception affects **motivation**, too. ADHD and some autistic brains are driven by:

1. **Intrinsic motivation** (tasks they genuinely care about).
2. **Near-term goals** (something in the immediate or short-term future).

Here's the problem:

- Tasks like studying or doing homework often lack immediate stimulation.
- Even if a student is motivated by a **long-term goal** (like earning a degree or dream job in three years), it's too far in the future to feel **real** and consistently motivate them.

This is why time perception issues make **time management** so difficult.

Why Time Feels Blurry (Past and Future)

ADHDers and some autistic people don't just experience blurry futures—**past events** are also difficult to place on a timeline.

Here's why:

- They may not intuitively "feel" how much time has passed since an event.
- Instead, they rely on **context clues** to estimate when it happened.

For example:

- "I was with this person at that time, so it must have been about 4 months ago because school started 4 months ago, and we haven't seen each other since then."

This lack of clarity applies to both the **past** and the **future,** creating challenges in organizing and planning around time.

What ADHDers and Autistic People Need

Support, understanding, and strategies tailored to their time perception are essential.

Here's how you can help:

- Encourage them to break tasks into **smaller, short-term goals**.
- Use **visual timelines or reminders** to make deadlines feel more tangible.
- Offer **presence and encouragement** to reduce overwhelm when the blurry future finally becomes clear.

Time perception issues aren't about carelessness—they're about how their brains are wired.

TL;DR:
- ADHDers and some autistic people have a **blurry sense of time**, both for the **past** and the **future.**
- **Far-off deadlines** feel intangible, making their brains behave as if they don't exist yet.
- They struggle with knowing when to start tasks or how long they'll take because time feels vague and abstract.
- Long-term goals don't consistently motivate them because they're too far away to feel real.

OTHER IMPORTANT TRAITS

In addition to executive functions, ADHDers and AuDHDers (autistic + ADHD) share other traits that are essential to consider when supporting a **neurodivergent child, student, or loved one.**

3

OBJECT PERMANENCE

The concept of **object permanence** was first discovered by child psychologist **Jean Piaget** and is a crucial milestone in early brain development.

It's the understanding that **an object continues to exist even when it can no longer be seen.** For example, babies who haven't yet developed object permanence might think their parent "disappears" during a game of peek-a-boo.

Object Permanence in ADHDers and AuDHDers

Here's where it gets interesting: ADHDers and AuDHDers don't believe unseen things cease to exist, but they momentarily **forget** they exist.

As the saying goes:

Out of sight, out of mind.

If something isn't directly in front of us, there's a good chance it will completely **slip from our minds.**

Everyday Examples of Object Permanence Challenges

For ADHDers and AuDHDers, this trait shows up in many aspects of life:

- **Tasks and projects:** If we put away a task or project to finish it later, we might not remember it until we randomly come across it again.
- **Interrupted work:** If we're interrupted mid-sentence while writing a paper, we might forget what we were going to say next.
- **Daily items:** We frequently lose our **keys**, **books**, or forget to put the **clothes in the dryer.**
- **Spaces:** Many of us maintain an "**organized chaos**"—keeping our surroundings messy on purpose to serve as **visual reminders** of things we need to do or were working on.

It's not that we're careless or lazy. It's that our brains literally **don't keep information in mind** once it's out of sight.

Object Permanence Applies to Ideas, Too

Object permanence isn't just about physical objects. It applies to **ideas.**

For example:

- When an ADHDer or AuDHDer has an idea (like remembering to buy shampoo or brainstorming a project), the worst thing they can tell themselves is:
  "I'll remember."
- **Spoiler alert:** They won't remember.

The solution?

- **Write it down.**
- **Tell someone.**
- **Set an alarm.**

Never trust your working memory to hold onto an idea, it's not designed for that.

Object Permanence and Relationships

Here's one of the most surprising twists about object permanence: it applies to **people** too.

ADHDers and AuDHDers can **forget about friends, family, or acquaintances** if those people aren't physically or consistently present in their daily lives.

This doesn't mean:

- They don't know who the person is.
- They don't care about them.

It just means those people **disappear from their mental radar** until something brings them back to the surface, like a text message, a memory, or a random association.

Object Permanence + Time Perception

When you combine **object permanence** with the ADHD/AuDHD brain's blurry **time perception**, you get scenarios like this:

- We think we talked to a friend **two weeks ago**, but in reality, it's been **six months.**
- We might feel certain that we've been keeping in touch, even when we haven't.

This often leads people to assume ADHDers and AuDHDers are **bad friends**, that they don't care because they don't reach out.

In reality, most ADHDers and AuDHDers **love their friends deeply** and are thrilled to reconnect, even after long gaps in communication.

A Message to Friends and Loved Ones

If someone with ADHD/AuDHD forgets to stay in touch, it's not because they don't care or value your relationship. Their brain just works differently:

- **Out of sight, out of mind** applies to people too.
- They still love and appreciate you, even if their actions don't always show it.

It's easy to take this personally, but it's rarely intentional. Showing patience and understanding can go a long way in maintaining strong connections.

TL;DR:

- **Out of sight, out of mind:** ADHDers and AuDHDers forget about tasks, objects, ideas, and even people if they're not physically present or immediately visible.
- Forgetting doesn't mean they don't care—it's just how their brains are wired.
- To keep track of ideas or reminders: **Write them down, set an alarm, or tell someone.**
- Object permanence challenges, combined with blurry **time perception**, make it easy to lose track of time and relationships.

4

ALL MANUAL

I magine what your life would be like if you had to **manually blink**. Every single time, you'd need to **notice** when you needed to blink and make the conscious **decision to do it.**

It would be exhausting and **draining**, right?

Fortunately, **blinking is automatic**, it's something the brain takes care of without us thinking about it.

ADHD EFs Are All Manual

Now, what if I told you that almost **everything neurotypical executive functions (EFs) do automatically**, like planning, organizing, and remembering ,must be done **manually** for ADHD brains?

And before you assume, this isn't because of a **deficit.** It's because **ADHD EFs are designed differently.**

ADHD EFs: Wired for Curiosity and Stimulation

ADHD brains are designed to be:

- **In the here and now.**
- Motivated by **curiosity, intellectual stimulation**, and **interest** (and sometimes, let's admit, **urgency**).

Here's what that looks like:

- ADHDers can **focus deeply**, but only on things that **spark curiosity** or **stimulation.**
- ADHDers can **undertake big projects**, like cleaning a room or learning a subject in one afternoon, but only when the task is **engaging** or **interesting.**
- ADHDers can **plan ahead**, but only when the goal feels **stimulating** or **exciting.**

If the task doesn't check one of these boxes, the ADHD brain has to rely on **manual effort** to make it happen, and that's exhausting.

What "Manual EFs" Look Like in Everyday Life

For someone with divergent EFs, **planning, organizing, prioritizing, remembering, and focusing** the way the school or work system demands is always a **conscious, manual action.**

It will **never become automatic.** It might feel more familiar with time, but it will always require **energy** and **intentional effort.**

Let's walk through an example:

A Day in the Life of "Manual EFs"

1. **Waking up:**

    ◦ You have to remind yourself of the **class schedule** for the day.
    ◦ Then, you manually search your memory: **Do I have anything to turn in? Did I even do the assignment? Where did I put it?**

    Just getting out of bed, without **curiosity or stimulation**, drains your **battery from 70% to 50%** before the day even starts. (By the way, many ADHDers and autistic people also struggle with **sleep**—we'll talk about that later.)

2.   **Getting ready for school:**

- You have to pause and manually remember: **Do I need my lunch? My transit pass? My supplies?**
- This isn't automatic, even if you've done it every day for years

3.   **In the classroom:**

- You have to spend energy staying **focused** and **engaged** with the teacher's lesson, even if it doesn't spark your curiosity.
- Then you realize you forgot an important item for class. You curse yourself for being "scatterbrained," lose confidence, and miss two minutes of teaching while you recover.

4.   **At the end of the day:**

- Your battery is at **20% or even 0%**, but you still have homework to do.
- School rarely sparks curiosity, intellectual stimulation, or interest because the structure and system are designed for neurotypical brains.

ADHDers and the School System

ADHDers are **highly intelligent**, but the traditional school system doesn't honor their cognitive strengths.

Instead of being encouraged to explore, think critically, or engage creatively, ADHDers are fed large amounts of information only to "vomit it back" on a page for an exam.

This isn't just **unengaging**, it's a **waste of their potential.**

TL;DR:

- For ADHDers, **executive functions** like planning, organizing, prioritizing, and focusing **are not automatic**.
- These tasks must always be done **manually**, requiring conscious effort and draining **energy** throughout the day.
- The school system rarely provides **curiosity, stimulation, or interest**, making it especially challenging for ADHDers to thrive.

5

PARALYZING

There are many situations that can leave an ADHDer or autistic person feeling **paralyzed**, unable to move or start even the smallest task.

From the outside, it might look like they're being **lazy** or unwilling to put in effort, but that couldn't be further from the truth.

Here's what's really happening:

1. Anxiety

For ADHD brains, which are constantly bombarded with **tens of thoughts at once**, anxiety can hit harder and faster than it does for neurotypicals.

When anxiety sets in, it can feel paralyzing, just like facing a lion in the wild. Even though **homework isn't a lion**, it can feel that way to an anxious brain.

Thoughts like:

- **"What if I don't understand the material?"**
- **"What if I fail, even though I studied?"**

These thoughts can be **scary**, and scared people **freeze.**

It's the brain's fight-or-flight system kicking in. Except, instead of fighting or running, the brain chooses **freeze.**

2. Overwhelm

Because ADHDers and some autistic people have to manually handle tasks like **planning, organizing, prioritizing, and problem-solving**, the mental load of approaching a task can quickly become **overwhelming.**

Imagine you've asked your computer to run 20 programs at once. The computer freezes, unable to process everything at the same time.

That's exactly what happens in an overwhelmed brain.

- Sometimes, the **mind goes blank.**
- Other times, the brain is so **loud** with competing thoughts that focus becomes impossible.

It's not laziness, it's cognitive overload.

3. Not Knowing Where to Start

One of the biggest sources of paralysis is **not knowing where to start.**

Imagine you've been given a recipe, but only **some steps** are listed.

- You might be able to guess that the oven needs to be set to **350°F** (because that's common in recipes).
- But if the ingredient list for the sauce is missing, there's **no way to know how to make it.**

For ADHDers and some autistic people, starting a task often feels like missing the recipe for the sauce. They simply **don't know what to do** or **where to start.**

Why "Simple" Tasks Aren't Simple

Let's take the example of **doing the dishes.**

For a neurotypical brain, "doing the dishes" feels like **one task.**

For ADHD-like executive functions, it's actually a **long list of tasks:**

1. Turn on the water.
2. Add soap.
3. Put silverware in the water.
4. Wash the silverware.
5. Rinse and dry.
6. Repeat with bowls.

It's like being handed 25+ **little papers** with each step written on them, but in no particular order.

Before they can even start the task, ADHDers have to **sort through the steps**, figure out the right order, and **then begin.** This is mentally exhausting and can lead to **paralysis**, especially if the brain views all steps as equally important (a common ADHD trait).

When someone says, **"It's just doing the dishes!"** they don't realize how much **manual effort** it takes for the ADHD brain to process all the steps.

When Paralysis Triggers Anxiety

Here's where things get even trickier:

- Seeing a pile of dirty dishes can trigger **anxiety** about the sheer number of steps involved.
- This anxiety can lead to **freezing**, which makes the task feel even more overwhelming, creating a cycle of paralysis.

Can It Get Easier Over Time?

Yes, repetition helps. The more ADHDers and autistic people perform a task, the more **familiar** it becomes.

But even when it becomes easier to navigate, the task still **isn't automatic.** It still requires **conscious effort** and **mental energy** to get started.

What They Need (Not Criticism, but Support)

When paralysis happens, what ADHDers and autistic people need most is:

- **Patience** and understanding.
- **Support** to break down the task into smaller, manageable steps.
- **Validation** that they're not lazy or incompetent—this is simply how their brain works.

Criticism only reinforces feelings of inadequacy, making paralysis worse.

4. When Things Aren't "As Usual"

When ADHDers and autistic people feel **safe and confident** in how they approach a task, it becomes familiar and scripted—almost like a mental **routine.**

But if **something changes**, the brain may **freeze** because:

- The task now feels **new**, and they don't know what to do next.
- It wasn't part of their "script," and we've already seen how new tasks can cause paralysis.

To neurotypical people, this might sound far-fetched:

- "If something changes, why not just adapt?"
- "Why not put in the effort to figure it out?"

But here's the truth:

- This **isn't something anyone has control over.**
- The **brain reacts automatically**, and while people can choose how to respond **after**, they can't stop the initial paralysis.

For ADHD-like executive functions, a small deviation can make the entire task feel unfamiliar, overwhelming, and impossible to start.

5. Waiting Paralysis

This form of paralysis is particularly **frustrating and disabling** because it often feels like a complete **waste of time.**

Here's what happens:

- ADHDers and some autistic people experience **distorted time perception.**
- If they have something planned later in the day, whether it's a meeting, appointment, or event, their brain struggles to start **anything else** beforehand.

Even if they technically have **plenty of time**:

- For example, they might have 3 hours before their appointment and know a task will only take 30 minutes.
- But to their brain, **30 minutes and 3 hours feel the same**, and the task still feels impossible to start.

So instead of doing the task, they end up **waiting**, unable to focus on anything else until the planned event is over.

While part of this is conscious ("I might not have enough time"), most of it is **subconscious**, driven by the ADHD brain's natural wiring.

6. The Inner Dialogue

One of the most **devastating causes of paralysis** is the harsh **inner monologue** many ADHDers and some autistic people live with.

Here's how it develops:

- Growing up, they often struggle to meet **family and school expectations** for planning, organization, focus, and follow-through.
- Without proper education about ADHD and executive functions, they internalize the belief that **they are the problem.**
- They're constantly told to "try harder" or "put in more effort," but even when they do, it's never enough.

Over time, this criticism takes a heavy toll on their **self-esteem** and **self-confidence.**

The "What's the Point?" Mindset

Years of feeling inadequate can lead to a defeatist attitude:

- **"What's the point? Even if I try, it won't be enough anyway."**

This mindset makes it harder to take control, find workarounds, or even attempt tasks they might otherwise manage. Instead of feeling supported, they feel:

- **Criticized, dismissed, and misunderstood.**

Rebuilding their confidence takes time, but what they need most is **understanding, encouragement, and support.**

TL;DR:

Many things can paralyze ADHDers and autistic people:

- **Anxiety:** "What if it doesn't work? What if I fail anyway?"
- **Overwhelm:** Too many steps at once, like a computer freezing.
- **Not knowing where to start:** All the steps hit at once, and they can't identify the first one.
- **When things aren't 'as usual':** If a task doesn't follow its usual "script," it feels like a brand-new task.
- **Waiting paralysis:** Distorted time perception makes it impossible to start another task while waiting for something planned.
- **Inner dialogue:** A harsh inner monologue tells them, "It's not worth trying—you'll fail anyway."

Paralyzed?

Some might think we use this word lightly, assuming it means "it's difficult to move."

But no, it's not "**difficult**". For many ADHDers and autistic people, it's simply **impossible.**

The Open Stove Analogy

Imagine you turn on the stove to the highest heat. The elements glow **bright red**, radiating heat. Someone promises you it won't burn you and they asks you to place your hand on it.

Physically, you have the capacity to do so, but your **brain won't let you.**

This is exactly what it's like for an **ADHD brain in paralysis.** Even if you're screaming in your head to **move,** to **put your foot on the floor,** or to **just do the thing,** your brain doesn't respond.

Now imagine living an entire life, especially a childhood, where you are criticized or punished for **not putting your hand on an open stove.**

With the stove, you KNOW why your brain refuses. You can tell yourself you have a valid reason. But with ADHD, especially with the **lack of education** surrounding it, you don't know why your brain won't cooperate. You really think there's a problem with you.

Can We Do Something About It?
Yes. Absolutely.

There are strategies and habits that can help fight paralysis:

- **Tips and tricks** can make planning and organizing easier.
- **Systems and structures** can help remind us of important things.
- While these changes will never make things **automatic,** they can make life more manageable.

But there's a catch:

- To make these changes, you need to address your **inner monologue** or have **safe people** around you for regular support.
- You cannot overcome paralysis simply by "making more effort."

Why "Effort" Doesn't Work

Here's the truth:

- Paralysis isn't caused by a **lack of effort**, so more effort won't fix it.
- It's like saying, **"I'm hungry, so I'll read a book."**
  - Reading won't satisfy your hunger—it's unrelated. You need to eat.
- And if you remember, ADHDers have difficuties "filling the blanks" so they simply don't know what "making more efforts" means, precisely.

Similarly, fighting paralysis requires addressing the **underlying issues**, not doubling down on effort that doesn't target the problem.

Fighting the Inner Monologue

One of the hardest parts of overcoming paralysis is silencing the **mean inner monologue** that has likely been with you since childhood.

Where Does It Come From?

This inner voice is a mix of:

- Your **parents' expectations**.
- Your **teachers' critiques**.
- Comments from **classmates**, **friends**, and even **media** messages.

Many ADHDers grow up believing:

- **"I'm not good enough."**
- **"I'll never meet expectations."**
- **"Why bother trying? It'll never be enough."**

Over time, this mindset takes a toll on **self-esteem** and **confidence**, leading to a sense of hopelessness and reinforcing paralysis.

For Parents of ADHD Kids

If you're a parent reading this book for your ADHD child, there's something important you can do right now:

You can help prevent these critical voices from taking root.

Why?

Because part of that inner monologue is shaped by **your voice.**

But don't feel guilty! Parenting a neurodivergent child is challenging, especially if you didn't know they had ADHD or didn't understand what

ADHD really meant. If you didn't know how their brain worked, how could you have known the right way to support them?

Instead of guilt, focus on learning, understanding, and **supporting them better now.**

For ADHD Adults Reading This

If you're an ADHDer adult looking for help with your studies or daily life, here's something to keep in mind:

Yes, part of your inner monologue may echo your parents' voices. But they were likely doing their best to **support and encourage you** in the only way they knew how.

If they didn't understand ADHD, they couldn't have known how to approach it effectively. Instead of holding a grudge, let's focus that energy on **fixing the present.**

Starting Your Healing Journey

Fighting the inner monologue isn't easy. For many, it requires **therapy** and a deep exploration of self-worth.

But you can start your healing journey today by:

- Learning more about **yourself** and how ADHD affects you.
- Understanding the **society** and **educational system** that shaped you.
- Developing strategies and systems that work **with your brain**, not against it.

This book will help you do all of that, so keep reading.

TL;DR:

- Paralysis isn't just "difficult"—it's often **impossible** to move or act, even when you're screaming at yourself to do so.
- Overcoming paralysis isn't about **effort**, because effort doesn't address the underlying problem.

- The mean **inner monologue**—a mix of voices from parents, teachers, and society—can make paralysis worse.
- Parents of ADHD kids can help by **avoiding harsh criticism** and offering **understanding and support.**
- For adults, starting your healing journey means understanding yourself, your brain, and the systems that shaped your experience.

6

WHY WE DON'T FINISH TASKS

I remember my parents lovingly teasing me about how I would never finish the projects I started. **Not finishing tasks** is a common experience for ADHDers and no, it's not because we're lazy or incapable.

There are **a few key reasons** why finishing can feel so difficult.

Dopamine-Driven Brains

As we've discussed earlier, the **ADHD brain is driven by dopamine**. Dopamine fuels our ability to **focus** on something or take **action** toward a goal.

When the brain **stops producing dopamine** about a particular project, it becomes incredibly hard to keep pouring energy into it. We might even **abandon the project entirely**, even if it was something we were **super excited about three weeks ago.**

It's important to understand that this isn't a **choice**. It's just how the ADHD brain works.

Now, it *is* possible to continue working on something even with less dopamine, but it's going to feel like trying to focus on a **boring school subject** that you just can't connect with. It takes **more energy** and effort, and that can feel overwhelming.

The Fear of Finishing

For some ADHDers, finishing a project isn't just hard, it's **scary.**

When we hyperfocus on something for weeks, months, or even **years**, that project can become a big part of our **identity**. So when we approach the **end of a project**, we might feel anxiety creep in:

- **Who will I be when this is done?**
- **How will I spend my time now?**
- **What comes next?**

The idea of closing this chapter can feel so overwhelming that it stops us from finishing altogether.

Normalizing Giving Up

Let me say this loud and clear: **It's okay to give up.**

If you've lost interest in a project or it no longer feels worth your time and energy, **there's no shame in letting it go.** Life is already stressful enough, and forcing yourself to finish something you don't care about anymore isn't always the best use of your resources.

But here's where it gets tricky: **Normalizing the idea that "ADHDers never finish anything"** can create its own set of problems.

If we internalize this stereotype, we might stop trying altogether. Instead of pushing through and finishing a project that could feel amazing to complete, we might give up simply because **"ADHDers never finish anything anyway."**

How We Can Support Finishing

By understanding why finishing is so hard for ADHDers, whether it's due to a **lack of dopamine** or the **fear of the end**, we can help them find ways to complete tasks that still **spark their interest.**

Sometimes, it's about finding a **new purpose** for the project. Other times, it's about offering support instead of assuming they won't finish anyway.

Not Linear

Let's clear something up: **it's not true that ADHDers never finish tasks or projects.**

ADHDers **do** finish things, but they might not do it in the **linear way** society expects. They might not work on a task **from start to finish** in one go.

Instead, they might return to their projects **weeks, months, or even years later**, when the **dopamine** comes back. They could switch between projects—**back and forth, here and there**—as a way to keep the dopamine flowing.

Different Wiring, Different Methods

Neurotypical people are used to working on **one thing at a time**, from beginning to end.

ADHDers, on the other hand, do it differently.

- They might tackle multiple projects in **alternation**, jumping between them as their interest shifts.
- They may need to pause and return later when the task becomes **exciting again.**

If ADHDers aren't teased or pressured about **"never finishing anything,"** they're much more likely to **return to their projects** on their own terms and finish them in their own time.

Why School Makes It Harder

Now, imagine asking an ADHDer to finish a project they're **not interested in**, and to complete it in **less than two weeks.**

It's easy to see why this is such a **challenge**. The **school system** wasn't designed for ADHD brains. It assumes everyone can:

- Sit down.
- Focus on one task.

- Follow a **linear timeline** from start to finish.

But for ADHDers, this structure **goes against how their brain is wired.**

TL;DR:
- ADHDers may not finish tasks the **traditional way** (from start to finish in one go).
- They often complete projects **later** or by switching between tasks to keep the **dopamine high.**
- Factors like **lack of dopamine**, the **fear of what comes next**, and **low expectations from others** can make it harder to finish.
- ADHDers **can finish things**—just in their own way and on their own timeline.

SO, WHAT IS ADHD?

7

SO, WHAT IS ADHD?

ADHD is a **neurotype** and a **neurodevelopmental condition**, meaning it's a condition that affects how the **brain and neurons develop**.

A **neurotype** refers to a type of **neurological pathway** that determines how the brain **perceives the world** and **processes information** from our senses and connections.

To be clear:

- **Neurotypical** is a neurotype.
- **ADHD** is a neurotype.
- **Autism** is also a neurotype, and, like ADHD, it's a neurodevelopmental condition.

Not a Disorder

Contrary to what we used to think, **ADHD and autism are not disorders.**

A **disorder** is a condition or illness that disrupts the **normal functioning** of something that's supposed to function a certain way. For a long time, we assumed that the **neurotypical brain** was the only "normal" neurotype, and anything that didn't match it was labeled a disorder.

But here's the thing: the way **ADHD and autism process information** is completely **normal** for their neurotype.

The Border Collie Analogy

Imagine a **border collie** running around and chasing sheep. This is completely **normal behavior** for that type of dog.

Now imagine asking your **chihuahua** doing the same thing. Would you say your chihuahua has a disorder just because it doesn't behave like a border collie?

Of course not! They're just **different types**, and their behavior is normal for what they are.

Similarly, **ADHD and autism** aren't disorders, they're just **different ways of being.**

Understanding Normal vs. Abnormal

To determine whether something is a **neurological disorder**, you need to compare it **to the same neurotype**, not a different one.

Here's an example:

- Until **1973**, **homosexuality** was listed as a disorder in the DSM (Diagnostic and Statistical Manual of Mental Disorders). It was seen as a **deviance** and "not normal."
- Today, we know that **homosexuality is normal.**

We're seeing the same shift with **neurodivergence**:

- We once thought it was "not normal."
- Then, as we discovered **different neurotypes**, we realized that **neurodivergence is just another type of normal.**

ADHD Has Always Been Here

ADHDers and autistic people have existed for as long as we've had records of human behavior. But their neurotypes were less noticeable in the past because life was so different.

For example, ADHDers and autistic people in history were often seen simply as:

- **Inventors, philosophers, creators, artists, and thinkers.**

Their neurodivergence they didn't know they had wasn't considered a problem—it was just part of who they were.

Science is Catching Up
While **ADHD and autism** are still labeled as **disorders** in the DSM-5, many voices in the psychological field are starting to claim otherwise.

Science takes a long time to change, but the truth is becoming clearer:

- **ADHD isn't broken, it's just different.**

ADHD and Executive Functions
ADHD is primarily about **differences in executive functions,** which, as we've seen, affect many aspects of daily life.

But ADHD isn't just about **attention deficits.**
In fact, the name "Attention Deficit Hyperactivity Disorder" is extremely misleading:

- ADHD is not a **deficit of attention.**
- Instead, it's more of an **attention variability**, where focus depends heavily on **dopamine, interest, and stimulation.**

A Better Name for ADHD?
Over the years, many people have proposed better names for ADHD, including:

- **DAVE** (Dopamine Attention Variability Executive-Functions).
- **Perierism** (from the Greek "periergos," meaning curious, and "ism," meaning state of being).

While no alternative name has replaced "ADHD" yet, these suggestions point to a deeper understanding of what ADHD actually is—a unique and valuable **neurotype.**

Looking Ahead

Now that we understand **what ADHD is,** we can shift our focus to the **world ADHDers have to navigate**—a world often designed with **neurotypical brains** in mind.

TL;DR:

- **ADHD is a neurotype, not a disorder.** Neurotypes are ways the brain processes information, and ADHD, autism, and neurotypical are all valid neurotypes.
- ADHD behaviors are normal for ADHD brains—just like running after sheep is normal for a border collie but not for a chihuahua.
- Science is beginning to shift its perspective, recognizing ADHD as different, not broken.
- ADHD is about **differences in executive functions** and **variability in attention**, not a deficit. The name "ADHD" is misleading, and many have proposed alternatives like **DAVE** to better capture its nature.

What About ADD?

For a long time, we believed there were two branches of the condition:

1. **ADHD** (Attention Deficit Hyperactivity Disorder),
2. And **ADD** (Attention Deficit Disorder, without hyperactivity).

Today, we know that **ADD doesn't exist** as a separate condition.

What we used to call **ADD** is now recognized as **ADHD inattentive type**. The "H" (hyperactivity) is always present—it just **doesn't express itself the same way** in every person.

ADHD is a Spectrum

Just like **autism is a spectrum**, **ADHD** is also a **spectrum.**
The **hyperactivity** in ADHD can manifest in **two ways**:

1. **Physical and cognitive hyperactivity,** or
2. **Cognitive hyperactivity only.**

Physical + Cognitive Hyperactivity

When hyperactivity is both **physical and cognitive**, it looks like the classic image of ADHD that most people think of:

- Someone who **talks a lot** and very **loudly.**
- **Constantly moving** or fidgeting, unable to stay still.
- Always seeking **stimulation** through activity.

This is the stereotypical picture of ADHD that people tend to recognize.

Cognitive-Only Hyperactivity

For many ADHDers, the **hyperactivity only happens in the brain.**

This is called **cognitive hyperactivity,** and it means their:

- **Inner monologue** never stops running.
- **Mind feels like chaos,** constantly juggling thoughts, ideas, and distractions.

Here's a popular meme that sums it up:

"Having ADHD is like having 50 tabs open on a browser, 3 are frozen, and you don't know where the music is coming from."

That's **cognitive hyperactivity.**

Why Inattentive ADHD is Underdiagnosed

From the outside, people with **inattentive ADHD** often:

- Appear **calm and quiet.**
- Don't move much or talk a lot.
- Seem like they're doing fine in school because they can sit still through classes.

But inside their heads? **It's chaos.**

Inattentive ADHDers struggle just as much as those with physical hyperactivity, but their challenges are often **invisible**. This makes them the most commonly **underdiagnosed** group.

They have the same **executive function challenges** as other ADHDers:

- Difficulty with planning, prioritizing, and focus.
- A need for **intellectual stimulation** to stay engaged.

Even though they might look like they're "managing" on the surface, **school and everyday life can still be incredibly difficult.**

TL;DR:
- There's no such thing as **ADD** anymore, it's all considered **ADHD.**
- ADHD can involve **physical and mental hyperactivity** or just **mental hyperactivity.**
- **Cognitive hyperactivity** feels like having 50 browser tabs open at once, with your mind running nonstop.
- Inattentive ADHD is often **misunderstood and underdiagnosed** because it looks calm on the outside, but inside, it's chaotic.

8

THE POSITIVE SIDE OF ADHD

While we've talked a lot about the challenges of ADHD, it's just as important to recognize the **amazing strengths** that often come with this neurotype. ADHDers bring unique skills, perspectives, and energy to the table, traits that can make them **innovators, creators, and leaders** in countless fields.

Let's take a closer look at some of the **hidden superpowers** of ADHD.

(I know, many don't like to think of their ADHD as a superpower, but while ADHD in itself can not be a superpower, some of the trait can be! Most non-ADHDers don't have them!)

Creativity

People with ADHD are natural outside-the-box thinkers. Their brains are wired to make **unexpected connections** and approach problems from **angles others might not even consider.**

This kind of creativity shines in fields like:

- **Art and design**, where unique perspectives spark innovation.
- **Technology and entrepreneurship**, where quick thinking and adaptability lead to groundbreaking ideas.

ADHDers thrive in roles that require:

- **Problem-solving under pressure.**
- Adapting to **fast-changing environments.**
- Finding **unconventional solutions** to tough challenges.

Their ability to see the world differently makes them valuable **team members** and **leaders**, bringing fresh ideas to the table and pushing projects in exciting new directions.

Hyperfocus

Hyperfocus is like a **superpower** for ADHDers. When something grabs their interest, they can:

- **Lock in completely,** shutting out all distractions.
- **Work at lightning speed**, achieving incredible results in a short amount of time.

It's like having a **supercharged laser beam of attention**, perfect for:

- Diving deep into **creative projects.**
- Learning **new skills** quickly and thoroughly.
- Solving **complex problems** that require intense focus.

In group settings, **hyperfocused ADHDers** often become the **go-to experts**, mastering details others might overlook. While hyperfocus can mean some tasks get left behind, when it's directed at the right thing, it can lead to **epic breakthroughs** and unmatched achievements.

High Energy

The energy of ADHDers is next level.
When they're working on something they're **passionate about**, this energy becomes a **powerful force** that helps them:

- Take on **big projects** without getting overwhelmed.
- **Push through challenges** that might tire others out.
- Tackle **new opportunities** with enthusiasm and drive.

In fast-paced environments, ADHDers thrive because they can **juggle multiple tasks** while staying engaged. This energy is perfect for **creative work**, allowing them to come up with **innovative solutions** and keep the momentum going.

Spontaneity and Adaptability

Quick thinking and flexibility are some of the ADHD brain's biggest strengths.
ADHDers excel in situations where:

- **Things change unexpectedly**, and plans need to shift.
- **Creative problem-solving** is required on the spot.

Their **spontaneity** makes them **naturals** at rolling with the punches, whether it's in **school, work, or everyday life.** They can handle surprises with confidence, adapt quickly, and find unique solutions that others might miss.

This adaptability helps ADHDers thrive in **unpredictable environments,** they bring fresh energy and creative ideas to whatever challenges come their way.

Curiosity

C uriosity is one of the greatest strengths of ADHD. People with ADHD often have an **endless drive to explore and learn.** Their love for discovery pushes them to dive into **new topics**, picking up knowledge in all kinds of areas, sometimes in ways others might never think to explore.

Whether it's **science, art, gaming, or something completely unexpected**, this curiosity can turn ADHDers into **multi-skilled pros.** They're constantly:

- **Chasing new ideas.**
- Thinking **outside the box.**
- Experimenting with **fresh perspectives.**

Their curiosity often leads to **innovative breakthroughs** and **creative solutions,** allowing them to excel in fields that reward a love for learning and a drive to try new things.

Problem-Solving Skills

B ecause ADHDers see the world **differently**, they bring a **unique approach** to solving problems.

Their ability to **think outside the box** allows them to:

- Spot **solutions** others might overlook.
- Come up with **creative strategies** to tackle challenges.
- Navigate tricky situations with a kind of **built-in GPS** for innovative thinking.

Whether it's:

- **Fixing something broken,**
- **Generating fresh ideas,** or
- **Facing a tough challenge,**

their ADHD brain's **different perspective** can lead to **amazing results.**

Need a fresh take on a problem? An ADHDer might just be your **secret weapon.**

Enthusiasm and Passion

When something truly grabs their attention, people with ADHD bring an energy that's hard to match.

Their **enthusiasm** is infectious, allowing them to:

- Dive into projects with **all their energy.**
- **Inspire others** with their excitement.
- Motivate a group to **rally behind an idea or cause.**

This passion can turn ADHDers into a **driving force** in any team. It's like having a **spark** that spreads, energizing those around them and fueling collaboration.

Whether it's:

- A **creative project,**
- A **new hobby,** or
- A **cause they care deeply about,**

their passion can make a huge impact, lifting the energy of the entire room.

ADHD Strengths in Action

These traits—**curiosity, problem-solving skills, and enthusiasm**—are just a few of the incredible ways ADHDers **shine in personal and professional settings.**

Given the right opportunities, these strengths allow ADHDers to:

- **Excel in creative fields.**
- **Thrive in fast-paced environments.**
- Bring **innovative ideas** and **new energy** to any team or project.

It's not just about managing ADHD, it's about recognizing the **superpowers** that come with it.

But, as with other forms of discrimination, **society has created categories to divide us. On one side, we hav**e **"neurotypi**cals," **the group of brains that society has decided are the "default." On the other side, there's everyone else : those of us who fall und**er **the broad umbrella term "neurodivergent."**

TL;DR:

ADHD isn't just about struggles—it comes with some **amazing strengths.**

- ADHDers are **super curious,** always exploring and learning new things.
- They bring **unique problem-solving skills,** finding creative solutions that others might miss.
- Their **enthusiasm and passion** are infectious, inspiring those around them to get excited too.

With the right opportunities, people with ADHD can turn their **unique perspectives and energy** into powerful tools that allow them to **thrive and succeed** in all areas of life.

9

A WORD ABOUT AUTISM

When it comes to **executive dysfunction**, there are similarities between ADHD and autism, but they're not exactly the same.

In ADHD, **executive dysfunction** is a **core trait**—it's central to the experience of ADHD and impacts almost everything.

In autism, **executive dysfunction** is more of a **secondary characteristic**. It often arises because of other traits of autism, like:

- **Sensory sensitivities.**
- **Hyperfocus** on specific tasks or topics.
- **Difficulty shifting attention** or adapting to change.

How ADHD and Autism Overlap

Both ADHD and autism involve differences in brain functioning, particularly in the **prefrontal cortex**, where executive functions are controlled.

But the **root causes** of these differences are distinct:

- **ADHD** is strongly tied to **dopamine dysregulation**, which affects motivation, focus, and impulse control.
- **Autism** involves differences in **neural connectivity** and **sensory processing**, which can indirectly affect executive functions.

The Autistic Brain: A Systematic Planner

Think of the **autistic brain** as a computer designed to thrive on **routine and structure**:

- When it's running on predictable processes, it's highly **efficient** and **detail-oriented.**
- But throw in an unexpected **pop-up window** (like a sudden change in plans), and the system might **slow down or crash momentarily.**

Key Traits of Autism Executive Functioning Differences

Here are some of the most common executive functioning traits in autism:

1. Cognitive Rigidity

Many autistic brains prefer **routine** and **predictability.** Sudden changes or switching between tasks can feel overwhelming—like asking a **Mac user** to navigate a **PC interface** without warning.

2. Hyperfocus Superpower

While ADHD often means **bouncing between tabs**, autism can lead to **intense hyperfocus** on one task or topic.

- This allows autistic people to dive **deep into their passions**, learning and mastering areas of interest.
- However, shifting attention to another task can feel like **dragging an anchor uphill.**

3. Overwhelmed by Multitasking

The autistic brain often excels at doing **one thing really well.**

- Multitasking, however, can feel like trying to **juggle ten windows** on a computer screen that wasn't designed for it.

4. Sensory Processing & Overload

Unlike ADHD, which is typically tied to **impulsivity**, autism often involves **sensory processing differences.**

- A chaotic environment—too **loud**, **bright**, or **overstimulating**—can make it nearly impossible to access executive functions effectively.

A Quick Comparison: ADHD vs. Autism Executive Functions

Executive Function	ADHD	Autism
Focus	Difficulty sustaining focus unless the task is **highly engaging**.	Tendency to **hyperfocus** on special interests, sometimes excluding other tasks.
Task Initiation	Paralyzed by **where to begin** or **how to start**.	Struggles to start tasks due to **unclear expectations** or **overwhelm**.
Cognitive Flexibility	Difficulty transitioning between activities, but often able to **adapt eventually**.	Strong preference for **routines**; changes can cause **significant distress**.
Emotional Regulation	Frequent **impulsive outbursts** or strong emotional reactions.	Emotional responses often tied to **sensory overload** or unexpected changes.

Executive Function	ADHD	Autism
Time Management	Struggles with **time blindness**, often underestimating or overestimating task length.	May **hyperfocus** and lose track of time entirely; routines help compensate.
Memory	Working memory is often **unreliable**, leading to forgetfulness and distraction.	May have **excellent memory** in specific areas, but short-term memory can falter in **complex, multi-step tasks.**

Why This Matters

Understanding the differences between ADHD and autism helps us better support both neurotypes. While they share **overlaps**, they require **different strategies** for managing executive functioning challenges.

For example:

- ADHDers may benefit from **dopamine-driven motivation tools**, like rewards or engaging tasks.
- Autistic people often thrive with **clear routines**, structured environments, and reduced sensory overload.

Recognizing these distinctions allows for **tailored support** that plays to each neurotype's strengths while addressing specific challenges.

Same Goals, Different Processes

Both **ADHD** and **autism brains** are **brilliant systems** designed to help people survive and thrive. However, their executive functioning operates on **different base codes**, which means they approach tasks in very **different ways.**

Let's take a simple example: **cleaning your room.**

The ADHD Brain: Starting is the Biggest Hurdle
For an **ADHD brain**, the challenge is often **getting started.**

- You might look at the **mess**, feel **overwhelmed**, and start bouncing between five different areas of the room.
- Half an hour later, the **laundry is half-folded**, the **bed is half-made**, and you're staring at a random box of stuff you meant to throw out—but hey, at least you found that cool thing you lost last month!

ADHDers often struggle with:

- **Task initiation** (Where do I even begin?).
- **Prioritizing steps** (What's the most important thing to tackle first?).
- **Staying on one task** (Oooh, shiny object!).

The Autistic Brain: Transitions Can Be the Hardest Part
For an **autistic brain**, the biggest hurdle might be **transitioning between tasks** or dealing with **unpredictability.**
Here's an example:

- You've got a **routine** for cleaning, so you're ready to tackle the laundry. But then someone suggests a **change in plans**—like moving the bookshelf instead. Suddenly, the system feels like it's **crashing** because the **unexpected change** wasn't part of the original plan.

However, once an autistic brain **starts a task**, their **focus and attention to detail** can be extraordinary.

- They might notice and fix **things no one else would.**
- The task may take longer, but the result can be **flawless.**

Both Systems Work—But in Different Ways

ADHD brains and **autistic brains** can both get the job done—but they take **very different routes** to get there.

The "Right-Click vs. Control+Click" Analogy

Let's imagine a neurotypical brain is like a **PC** with a **right-click function.** ADHD and autism brains are more like **Macs**—they have their own **unique commands** and shortcuts. And you can smash the "right-click" button on a Mac mouse, that won't do anything. That's pretty much using a neurotypical tool for and ADHD brain.

For ADHD Brains:

The struggle is often about **finding the right shortcut to get started.**

- It might feel like you're **clicking all over the desktop**, opening and closing windows, but never launching the program you actually need.
- However, once you find that **shortcut**—like breaking the task into smaller steps, setting a timer, or listening to music—you can **lock in and get things done.**

It's like hitting **Command+Space** on a Mac to open Spotlight Search. Once you're there, you can finally type in what you need and make progress.

For Autistic Brains:

The process might involve **adjusting for compatibility.**

- Imagine someone hands you **software built for a PC** (a neurotypical task with unclear instructions). It may take **extra time** to figure out how to run it on your Mac.
- But once you've found a way, your execution can be **incredibly precise**—sometimes even **more efficient** than the original plan.

Why This Matters

Understanding the differences in **executive functioning** between ADHD and autism is essential because it shows **why the same tools and strategies won't work for everyone.**

For ADHD Brains:

Telling an ADHD brain to **"just try harder"** is like telling a Mac to **right-click**. It's not about effort—it's about finding the **right process** that works with their wiring.

For Autistic Brains:

Asking an autistic brain to **"just go with the flow"** is like expecting a carefully planned program to **adapt to a glitch**. It's not about resistance—it's about needing the **tools and time** to process the change.

The Strengths of Both Neurotypes

Both ADHD and autism brains bring **incredible strengths** to the table:

- ADHD brains excel in **creativity, energy, and adaptability.**
- Autistic brains shine in **focus, precision, and attention to detail.**

To thrive, these neurotypes need **understanding, flexibility**, and the **right accommodations**—not one-size-fits-all solutions.

TL;DR:

- ADHD and autism brains approach tasks differently because of their unique **executive functioning challenges.**
- **ADHD struggles** with impulsivity, task initiation, and time management, while **autism struggles** with task-switching, cognitive flexibility, and sensory overload.
- Neurotypical tools don't always work—ADHD needs **dopamine-driven strategies** to get started, while autism benefits from **clear routines and predictable steps.**
- Embrace the strengths of each neurotype by working **with their operating system, not against it.**

THE CAPITALISM INFLUENCE

Wait! Don't close the book just because we're mentioning the "**bad bad capitalism.**" This isn't just about corporations and profits, it's about how the **capitalist mindset** shapes the school system.

More importantly, it's about how this system can negatively impact an **ADHD student**, or honestly, **any student**. Capitalism's influence on education goes beyond the classroom and into the **core values** of how schools operate.

10

FROM THE EARLY AGE

From the Very Beginning

Let's start with this: **school is good.** Education is essential. Providing a **general education** to an entire population is critical for the **healthy growth of any society.**

No matter what kind of society or government exists, **schools have always been there** in some form.

- It could be an elaborate **national system** or an **improvised village classroom**.
- Even in places where resources are scarce and children may never set foot in a classroom, the **concept of school and learning** exists almost everywhere on the planet.

The **idea of mandatory education** is inherently **positive and selfless**: to provide **everyone** with a foundation of **basic knowledge** that helps them navigate life.

The Capitalist Mindset in Education

But here's where capitalism changes things. In a **capitalist society**, the focus is on:

- **Productivity.**
- **Competition.**
- Getting things done **quickly and efficiently.**

And this mindset **seeps into the education system.**

What was originally designed to teach children **how to think and grow** now puts emphasis on **output over process**:

- How much can you achieve in the shortest amount of time?
- How well can you compete with others?
- How do you prepare students to enter a workforce that values **efficiency** over **creativity or individual growth?**

These priorities affect the way schools are structured, the way students are evaluated, and the way success is defined.

Why This Matters for ADHD Students

This capitalist influence doesn't just hurt ADHD students—it creates a system that's **detrimental to any student** who doesn't naturally fit the mold.

For ADHD students, in particular, the emphasis on **standardized outcomes**, **competition**, and **speed** creates unique challenges:

- ADHD brains don't function based on **external deadlines or rigid systems**; they're motivated by **interest, curiosity, and stimulation.**
- A system that rewards students for being **linear thinkers** or **fast executors** is the exact opposite of what ADHDers need to thrive.

The result? ADHD students are often:

- **Labeled as "lazy" or "unmotivated"** when their brains simply aren't wired for this approach.
- Forced into an **environment** that highlights their challenges instead of their strengths.

Education Shouldn't Be About Output

The capitalist influence shifts education away from its true purpose: to **nurture curiosity, foster growth**, and prepare students to **think critically about the world.**

Instead, it turns school into a **factory model** where students are expected to:

- Learn at the **same pace**,
- Produce the **same results**, and
- Compete against one another in ways that may leave some students behind.

For students with ADHD (and many others), this creates **barriers** rather than opportunities.

But **education doesn't have to be like this**. By understanding how **capitalist values** shape the system, we can start to think about **alternatives** that allow all students to thrive, regardless of their neurotype.

Smarter Than the Others

From a young age, we've been immersed in a school system that measures us by **grades** and uses them to rank our knowledge and skills. As early as **five years old**, we're taught that success is tied to **test scores**—concrete, tangible markers of how well we've done.

It's hard to avoid comparisons in this kind of system. After every test, the top students eagerly ask, **"What did you get?"** Success feels rewarding—outperforming others gives you a sense of pride, makes you feel **smart**, even like a "better" person.

But there are two major things we need to rethink when it comes to intelligence and grades.

What Is Intelligence, Really?

The first misconception is that intelligence is about **grades**. From a young age, we're taught that "smart people" are the ones with the **high-**

est scores and that intelligence leads to better jobs, more success, and a brighter future.

But that's **not true.**

The ability to **memorize information** for a test isn't the same as **intelligence.** True intelligence is about how well you can **think, reason, reflect, and adapt** to new situations. It's the ability to make **logical connections** between ideas and **deduce solutions** from the information you have.

For example, in math classes, teachers often care more about seeing your **reasoning** than just the final answer. If your reasoning is logical, even if the answer is wrong, you'll still get points. This is because **critical thinking** and the ability to make connections are far more valuable than simply memorizing formulas.

This kind of thinking is essential in today's world. With the internet bombarding us with **information and misinformation**, **critical thinking** is what helps us evaluate what's true, what's false, and how to respond.

Intelligence is also **much broader** than we often give it credit for. There are many types of intelligence: **spatial, musical, emotional, and more.** Intelligence isn't just about knowing facts, it's about awareness, creativity, and problem-solving.

ADHDers, Autistics, and the Struggle with Grades

For people with ADHD or autism, their intelligence is often tied to **interest.** If a subject doesn't grab their attention, they may struggle to retain information and perform well on tests.

But when something **does** catch their interest, their brains dive in with incredible focus and enthusiasm. They can quickly become **experts** on topics they love, learning deeply and creatively.

Some ADHDers and autistic people excel in school because **learning itself** is one of their passions. For many others, though, traditional school systems create a constant battle, and they need **support and ac-**

commodations just to keep up. This isn't because they're not intelligent, it's because the system isn't designed for how their brains work.

Grades Don't Define Intelligence

Doing well on written tests doesn't mean someone is **smarter** or more **capable.** It simply means they've mastered a specific skill: recalling information on paper in a structured format.

Yes, intelligence can make it easier to learn and remember things, especially when you can create **logical links** between pieces of information. But intelligence and **learning-by-heart** are two **very different things.**

A Flawed Measure of Intelligence

The best way to measure intelligence is through **sophisticated psychological tests** that account for various types of intelligence, from logical to emotional to creative. Yet in schools, we rely almost entirely on **grades**—and these are a flawed way to gauge intelligence.

Grades only show how well someone can answer questions the way the **teacher expects.** They don't account for how a student might interpret the question differently or how they might arrive at a correct answer in an unconventional way.

This makes written tests an **unreliable** measure of intelligence. They miss the bigger picture: the ability to adapt, think critically, and create new ideas.

Why Growth Is Praised More Than Excellence

The second problem with the grading system is how we value **improvement** over **consistency.**

Imagine a student who improves from a **C to an A**. They're often praised and celebrated for their growth, and rightly so. But now think about the student who earns **As consistently**. Their achievement is just as impressive, requiring sustained effort and mastery. Yet, they're less likely to be noticed or praised because their success is **expected.**

This imbalance creates a **skewed perception of achievement.** Improvement is visible, but **maintaining excellence** often goes unnoticed. Both should be recognized for what they are: evidence of effort, dedication, and growth.

Rethinking Intelligence and Success

We need to challenge the idea that grades are the best indicator of **intelligence** or **potential.** A high score on a test doesn't necessarily mean someone is more competent or capable in the real world.

Intelligence is about far more than **memorizing facts.** It's about thinking critically, solving problems, and adapting to new challenges.

ADHDers and autistic people, in particular, show us that intelligence doesn't always fit neatly into the boxes defined by traditional education. By recognizing **different kinds of intelligence** and appreciating the **effort behind both growth and consistency**, we can create a more meaningful and inclusive way of valuing people's abilities.

TL;DR:

Grades don't define intelligence, and memorizing facts isn't the same as being smart. **True intelligence** is about critical thinking, reasoning, and making connections. ADHDers and autistic people are often highly intelligent but need engaging, stimulating subjects to thrive—something that grades rarely reflect.

The education system values **memorization, routines,** and **sitting still,** which don't align with how ADHD brains are wired. This can make it easy to feel like you're not smart, but nothing could be further from the truth.

ADHDers are incredibly **creative**, with an unmatched ability to **think outside the box** and spot **connections others might miss.** They excel in ways that don't fit the school mold, like solving problems on the spot or diving deep into subjects they love. Unfortunately, these strengths often go **unrecognized** because traditional classrooms aren't designed to showcase them.

Intelligence isn't about grades, it's about **how you create, think, and approach the world.** If school has ever made you feel less than, remember: the system wasn't built to measure your kind of brilliance. Your **creativity, passion,** and unique perspective will thrive where traditional metrics fall short.

Comparing to Others

From a young age, we're taught to **compare ourselves to others**, especially when it comes to school. Students often look to those struggling to feel better about themselves, while adults, teachers and parents, push comparisons with those excelling, saying things like, **"If student A can get a good grade, so can student B."**

But let's be real: it's **not that simple.**

The Habit of Comparison

By the time students reach high school, this habit of **comparing to those doing better** is deeply ingrained. And since there will always be someone ahead, they begin chasing **unreachable goals**, reinforcing the belief that they're never good enough. This damages their **self-love, self-esteem,** and **self-confidence.**

This cycle is especially harsh for ADHD students, or worse, undiagnosed ADHD students, who struggle to:

- Focus in class.
- Retain information for tests.
- Complete papers in the way the system demands.

When you're constantly compared to peers who seem to easily absorb and reproduce information, it's hard not to feel **stupid or behind.** But here's the truth:

You're **not stupid.** The **school structure** just isn't built for the way your brain works, and many students never receive the **accommodations** or **support** they need.

Why Comparison to Non-ADHDers Doesn't Work

Comparing yourself to neurotypical classmates is like comparing **cucumbers to oranges.**

- Their brains are wired differently.
- They might focus easily or finish tasks quickly, while your ADHD brain might need **more time**, **systems,** or **structure** to stay on track with tasks that don't naturally spark your interest.

This doesn't mean you're less capable, it means you **operate differently.**

What you *can* do, though, is focus on your **own progress.** While a neurotypical person might struggle to focus for hours on one topic, your ADHD brain might thrive in a subject you're passionate about. **Your strengths are different**, but they're just as valuable.

Shifting the Perspective

Comparing yourself to others isn't always a bad thing, but it has to be done **in balance.** Most of us only look at those doing better, completely ignoring the fact that we're **ahead of others** in some ways, too. This skewed perspective shapes our identity, often overshadowing our achievements and diminishing our self-worth.

To break this cycle, start by **acknowledging your progress.** Recognize your unique journey and remind yourself that everyone has **different strengths and struggles.**

We're not robots, we're human. We're all born with a different set of **skills** and **challenges.** And while difficulties can be worked on, they require **time**, **support**, and **encouragement.**

Celebrate Your Wins

When you compare yourself to others who don't face the same obstacles, it's easy to feel frustrated or like you're falling behind. But you're not living the same reality as them. Your journey is your own.

Instead of focusing on where others are, **celebrate your small wins.** They're a big deal. Progress, no matter how slow or small, deserves to be appreciated.

TL;DR:

Comparing yourself to others, especially when you have ADHD, is often unfair and unproductive. Focus on **your growth**, appreciate the unique strengths you bring to the table, and remember that **everyone's path is different.** What works for them might not work for you, and that's okay. **You're doing your best, and that matters.**

It Starts in Kindergarten

Imagine this. From the very beginning, **we train young minds** to compare themselves to others. Since kindergarten, kids are taught to **compete** for the best grades, or what they believe are markers of being the **"smartest,"** the **"best,"** or even a **"better person."** Faster, smarter, ahead in life.

But as we said: the ability to **learn, retain,** and **understand information** is different for everyone. Each person learns in their **own way.** Some are **visual learners**, others are **auditory** or **kinesthetic.** Some people naturally have better memory than others, and guess what?

None of this has anything to do with intelligence.

A System That Doesn't Fit Everyone

The school system, unfortunately, **teaches in only one way**:

- Subjects are explained in a **single format,**
- Tests are conducted in **writing,**
- All students are evaluated **together, at the same time, in silence.**

It's a rigid system that **clearly doesn't fit every student.**

Think about this: If students were evaluated **one-on-one** with their teacher, verbally, **many would perform far better.** A discussion format would allow students to **express their understanding** in a way that suits them. Teachers could better evaluate their knowledge without relying solely on written tests.

Knowledge vs. Intelligence

To **know a lot** of facts is simply to have **a lot of knowledge,** not intelligence. By the same token, someone can be **highly intelligent** but struggle with **memorizing information** or learning things by heart.

We need to let go of the **false belief** that doing well in the **school system = intelligence.** The ease of learning in a classroom context is not a measure of how smart someone is. **It's not that simple.**

> ## Parenthesis: School ≠ Real Life
> Let's pause here for an important point.
>
> Getting straight As in school doesn't necessarily reflect your abilities as a worker, or even as a person. It doesn't show how resourceful you are, how well you can adapt, or how effectively you can work with others. It just means you fit well within the current school system and are good at absorbing information in a specific way.
>
> But the real world is nothing like school. Being top of your class doesn't automatically mean you'll excel in the workplace or in life. Success in school doesn't always translate to success in the workforce or the world beyond it. And that's okay.

School Mirrors Workforce Values

Since kindergarten, we've been **compared to our classmates,** and we start to evaluate our **self-worth** based on grades.

School is important, yes, but the way it's structured often reflects what's expected of a **good worker** rather than a curious learner. The focus on grades and tests mirrors the values of **productivity** and **measurable success** that are celebrated in the workforce.

Just as we're rewarded in school for **better grades** or **consistent excellence**, the workplace rewards those who continually **improve** or **excel.** The system is designed to prepare students for this kind of world, but not necessarily for a world that celebrates different kinds of intelligence, creativity, or learning styles.

The Weight of Validation

The school system's **focus on measurable outcomes** often overshadows the value of **creativity, critical thinking,** and **emotional**

intelligence. Students are pressured to perform and compete, stifling their individuality and teaching them to equate success with **external validation.**

This mindset doesn't stop at school. In both academics and the workplace, steady, consistent effort is often overlooked in favor of **dramatic improvements** or **big achievements.** Over time, this creates a cycle where a person's **sense of worth** becomes tied to their performance, leading to **burnout** and a constant need for approval from others.

A System That Shapes Lives

We are literally creating young people who constantly seek **validation from others** and let society's opinions dictate their decisions and self-worth. **We taught them this.**

Both **capitalist society** and **family expectations** play a huge role in fostering this behavior. The system prioritizes productivity and comparison over individuality, encouraging students to focus on **how they're ranked** rather than how they feel or think.

Navigating School with ADHD

For students with ADHD, this culture of **comparison** can be especially tough. The school system indirectly teaches children to measure themselves against their classmates. If you're an ADHDer, you might look at your peers, those who seem to "have it all together", and wonder why you're struggling.

Here's the truth: they don't have it all together. They just have brains that fit the school system better than yours does.

The Impact of Undiagnosed ADHD

It gets even harder if you don't know you have ADHD. Without a diagnosis, you might not understand why things that seem **easy for others**, like sitting still, staying focused, or remembering information, feel **so hard for you.**

This can lead to feelings of inadequacy, as you start to believe that you're just **not as smart or capable** as your classmates. Because in your mind, you should be just like them, because you don't know you are not neurotypical.

A Different Mold

If you're struggling, it's not because you're **not good enough.** It's because the system isn't designed to play to your **strengths.** Once you understand how your brain works, you can start finding **strategies that work for you.**

You don't have to fit into a mold that was **never built with you in mind.** You can succeed by creating a system that values your strengths instead of forcing yourself into one that highlights your struggles.

TL;DR:

From kindergarten, we're trained to compare ourselves to others based on grades, equating success with intelligence. But the **one-size-fits-all school system** doesn't suit everyone, especially ADHDers. Intelligence isn't about memorizing facts—it's about **creativity** and **critical thinking.** This emphasis on grades mirrors the workplace's focus on productivity, leading to **external validation** becoming a measure of self-worth.

The system wasn't built for ADHD brains, but you can create one that celebrates your strengths instead of trying to fit into a mold that doesn't.

11

THE CAPITALIST SOCIETY

It's normal to want to feel **recognized**, **loved**, and **validated.** Humans are social creatures, **gregarious by nature.** We thrive in groups, relying on the **presence** and **recognition** of others to feel fulfilled.

Even the most confident and self-assured person still needs **connection** and **affirmation** from others. It's part of what makes us human.

But in a **capitalist society,** this natural human need for recognition is manipulated.

Capitalism and Identity

Capitalism isn't just about **money** or **work.** It's about shaping people into **workers first**, humans second. When your **identity** becomes tied to your job, you start to prioritize work over everything else: your **mental health,** your **leisure time,** and even your **personal growth.**

This system thrives on making people **hyper-focused on productivity.** By constantly "going the extra mile," you end up working so much that, when you finally get home, you're too **exhausted** to do anything but relax.

There's no time or energy left for **self-reflection**, for example, to stop and think about whether this lifestyle is even healthy. Instead, you just accept it. You tell yourself, **"That's life. It is what it is."**

But Is That Really Life?

Here's something to think about: When you meet someone new, whether in a group or online, what's one of the first things you tell them about yourself?

You probably mention your **job** or your **field of study.**

Why is that? Why do we so often lead with what we do for work?

The answer lies in how deeply **capitalism** has shaped our sense of identity.

What's Next?

Understanding this dynamic is the first step toward questioning it. Why do we tie so much of our self-worth to productivity? How can we redefine success in ways that prioritize our humanity over our output? Well, two reasons.

First, **Social Worth.**

In our society, your **job** is often seen as the foundation of your **worth.** And how does a capitalist society measure worth? **Money.** The more you earn, the more valuable you are considered.

If you're unemployed, people might **look down on you** or even call you **lazy.** But if you're a **doctor, lawyer,** or **business owner,** you're suddenly worthy of **respect.** Taking time off to care for yourself or pursue something different? Be ready to explain that **"gap in your resume."**

Validation Through Work

Having a **good job** or a **university degree** is treated as the ultimate form of **validation.** It's seen as society's way of saying, "You're capable, intelligent, and successful." The problem is that these are often the **only things** that are valued.

Without recognition from our friends, family, or partners for **who we are,** our qualities, kindness, or personal achievements, we begin to define ourselves solely by our **jobs, grades,** and **academic success.**

But here's the truth: we are so much more than our **professional titles** or **GPA.**

The Pressure to "Stand Out"

From a young age, we're pressured to **stand out**, to get the **best grades**, to attend **university** (because, of course, **"some random college"** isn't good enough), and to secure a "prestigious" job. Why? Because **academics are praised** as intelligent, capable, and strong.

And since society often doesn't value other forms of success, many of us chase this narrow path, even when it doesn't align with who we are.

As Jonathan Louis Dent once said:
"Imagine if we measured success by the amount of safety that people felt in our presence."

Let's go further: **Imagine if we measured a person's worth, not by how much money they made, but by how safe, seen, and cared for others felt when they were around.**

A Shift in Perspective

Thankfully, more and more people are realizing how **toxic** this mindset is. Many now aspire to simply have a **job they enjoy**, make **enough money to live,** and actually **enjoy life.**

But here's the hard truth: everything in our society—from schools to workplaces—is designed to teach us, starting in **kindergarten**, how to become **obedient workers.**

Capitalism and ADHD

Capitalism can be especially tough for people with **ADHD**, and here's why: it places a high value on **productivity, efficiency,** and the ability to **focus for long periods.** But those traits? They aren't always the strengths of someone with ADHD.

ADHDers often excel in areas like **creativity, problem-solving,** and **thinking outside the box.** But these strengths aren't always recognized in a system that rewards grinding through **repetitive tasks** or following **rigid routines.**

When your worth is measured by how much you can **produce** or how well you can stick to the "rules," it's easy to feel like you're always **falling short.**

A System That Doesn't Fit

The truth is, capitalism wasn't built to celebrate ADHD brains. It's like trying to fit a **square peg into a round hole**—no matter how hard you try, the system isn't designed to accommodate you.

But here's the important part: that doesn't mean **you're not valuable.** Your worth isn't determined by a system that can't see your strengths.

Your value is in how you **think, create,** and approach the world in a way that others can't.

TL;DR:

Society often bases our worth on how much money we make. Prestigious jobs bring respect, while not working leads to judgment. But more people are starting to realize how toxic this mindset is, shifting their focus to enjoying life and doing meaningful work. For ADHDers, capitalism's emphasis on productivity and rigid systems doesn't highlight their unique strengths, but that doesn't make them less valuable. Your worth isn't tied to your output—**it's tied to who you are.**

Identity

When introducing ourselves, we often start by sharing what's most **central to our lives**—what we identify with most. If your **job** or **field of study** is one of the first things you mention, it's likely become a **significant part of your identity.**

"But that's normal! I love what I do—it's part of me!"

Yes, your **interests** and passions are part of who you are. But your **job** is still just that—**a job.**

Saying **"I love mechanics"** reflects what excites you, but saying **"I'm a mechanic"** makes it your **identity.** And yes, being a mechanic is a part of you, but you're also so much more. You might be a parent, a geek, a sports enthusiast, an artist, or someone who loves walking in the woods, music, and concerts. You are a combination of your **passions, quirks, and roles,** not just your profession.

The Danger of Tying Identity to Work

When your **job** becomes the **core of your identity**, it can have harmful effects. You may begin to define your **self-worth** entirely through your **work achievements** or **productivity.**

When things are going well at work or school, you might feel great. But when they're not? That's where the problem lies. Any setback or failure can feel like a **personal failure**, leading to **burnout** and a distorted sense of self.

You Are More Than Your Job

Loving what you do is wonderful, but it's important to recognize that your job is **just one piece of the puzzle.** You are so much more than your work or your academic success. By embracing your **other roles, passions,** and **qualities**, you can build a healthier sense of self that doesn't rely entirely on productivity or external validation.

TL;DR:

When we introduce ourselves, we often start with our jobs, making them a big part of our identity. While loving your work is great, your job is just **one part** of who you are. You're also a parent, a geek, a sportsman, an artist, and much more. Defining yourself by your job can be toxic, tying your worth to work achievements and leading to burnout. **Remember, you are more than just a worker or a student.**

Performance-Driven Society

We live in a world where your **worth** feels tied to how much you can **perform.** Where you're constantly pushed to **outdo yourself** just to feel valued.

Let me repeat that.

Your **worth as a human being** is tied to how much you **perform.**

This is deeply problematic.

The Pressure to Perform

Teenagers, in particular, face overwhelming pressure just to earn a little recognition. By the time they're **16 or 18**, many are struggling with **high anxiety** and **low self-esteem.** And we, as a society, are to blame.

We've taught them that their **value** comes from grades, achievements, and validation. They push themselves to make their **parents proud** and to meet **society's standards,** but this is exactly what a capitalist system wants. It doesn't care about their well-being; it wants **workers**—people who will carry the mindset of **"strive harder, produce more"** into adulthood and the workplace.

Even if you're someone who doesn't care about academic recognition, you're stuck in a system where **grades open or close career doors.** University and job requirements set the rules for what success looks like, and there's no escaping it.

When a door closes, **even one you never planned to walk through,** it can feel like the **end of the world.** At 19, you might already feel like you've missed your chance at success.

Redefining Success

We need to define **success differently.**

Success should be about how much you **help others,** how you **better the world,** and how you **grow as a person.** It shouldn't just be about grades, degrees, or promotions.

But from the moment we're young, we're fed the idea that **performance equals worth.** It starts as early as **daycare** and becomes the focus of life by kindergarten: **School, homework, lunch, bath, bedtime. Repeat.**

Young children are praised for **good grades** and reprimanded for **poor ones**, as if making a mistake or struggling is something to be **ashamed of.**

School quickly becomes the **center of life**, with weekends and vacations feeling like the only chance to breathe. By the time many students reach high school, they don't even know who they are outside of academics.

Knowing Yourself

What's missing from this system is something just as important as academics: the chance to **know yourself.**

School teaches us to memorize **dates** and **math formulas** we'll rarely use again. And even if we do need them in the future, we'll be taught them again. But it doesn't teach us to:

- Understand our **values.**
- Identify our **strengths, fears,** and **abilities.**
- Reflect on why certain activities energize us while others drain us.
- Develop critical thinking and **self-respect.**

Knowing yourself isn't just about preferences. It's about truly understanding your emotions, your boundaries, and what drives you.

The ADHD Perspective

For ADHDers, this system is especially damaging. School is structured to produce **obedient workers** who can sit still, follow rules, and work in repetitive ways. But ADHDers aren't wired that way—they're **inventors** and **creators.** I know I feel like a broken record, but it's so important to not only being aware of it, but to seeing it too.

Their strength lies in **thinking differently**, but they're forced to **adapt every single day** to a system that goes against their nature. Over time, this constant need to adapt can take a serious toll, leading to exhaustion and a sense of never measuring up.

TL;DR:

We live in a performance-driven society that ties our worth to how much we can achieve. This pressure starts in childhood, teaching us to value grades and productivity over creativity, self-awareness, and personal growth. Teenagers, especially, face immense stress, leading to anxiety and low self-esteem. For ADHDers, this system is even more harmful because it forces them to adapt in ways that go against their nature. We need to redefine success to focus on **good deeds, helpfulness,** and **self-discovery**, not just academic or work achievements.

Second, **Family.**

Family plays a huge role in the **pressures** young people feel. As children, we instinctively look to our parents for **validation** and **approval.** That's normal—it's part of being human.

And, of course, most parents want what's **best** for their kids. They want their child to have every **opportunity** to succeed, to keep as many **doors open** as possible, so they can land a job they'll be happy in.

Grades and Parental Approval

From elementary school onward, **grades** often become the foundation of this approval.

When we bring home good grades, most parents are **happy** and sometimes even **proud enough to brag** about their child's success. But when grades are bad? That's where the pressure comes in. Reprimands like **"you could have done more"** or **"you won't get into university like that"** start to surface.

And we believe them, of course. They're our parents. They're supposed to know what they're talking about.

When Parents Miss the Mark

Unfortunately, many parents don't respond to bad grades with the **empathy** their child truly needs. Instead of saying something like, **"What happened? How can I help? I know you did your best,"** they might focus on the failure itself, unintentionally adding to their child's stress and feelings of inadequacy.

This is especially true for kids with ADHD.

From my experience working with ADHDers, I've found that most parents still believe it's just a matter of **"effort"** andthat their child could do better if only they tried harder. This misunderstanding stems from a lack of **education about ADHD.**

It's not their fault, **education about ADHD** is neither up-to-date nor widely available. Most parents simply don't know what ADHD is or how to support their child better. And you can't act on what you don't know.

That's part of why I wrote this book: to help parents understand, so they can become the **safest, most supportive** people in their child's life.

Pressure Without Words

Even when parents don't openly comment or criticize, their reactions can still **condition us.** As kids, we're constantly observing the people around us, picking up on their behaviors and responses.

Maybe you're four or six years old, watching your mom sigh when she hears about your older brother's bad grades. Or maybe your dad beams with pride when he congratulates your cousin on her academic success.

You might not be directly told anything, but your little brain is still making **connections**:

- "I don't want to disappoint Mom with bad grades."
- "I want Dad to feel proud of me too."

Even without meaning to, parents can create a sense of **pressure.** The intention is never to harm, but kids are incredibly perceptive, and they internalize what they see and hear.

The result? We start putting **pressure on ourselves.** We strive for the best grades—not necessarily because our parents asked us to, but because we've learned that it's the path to **approval** and **love.**

TL;DR:

Parents play a big role in the pressure kids feel to succeed. Good grades are often met with pride and approval, while bad grades bring reprimands. For ADHDers, this can be especially tough since many parents still view academic struggles as a lack of effort rather than a reflection of how their child's brain works. Even without direct criticism, children pick up on subtle cues from their parents, conditioning themselves to strive for success to earn love and approval. The goal is for parents to become informed, empathetic, and the safest source of support for their kids.

Validation, Pride, and Recognition

From the moment we're born, **validation** comes from the people around us long before it comes from within. As children, we instinctively seek our parents' **approval** and **pride.** Seeing them happy with us feels like proof that we're **worthy.** It **validates who we are** and what we're capable of.

The Pressure to Fulfill Their Dreams

One of the things I find troubling is how, as parents, we often push our children to **finish their studies quickly,** find a **"good job,"** and be settled in life by **25.**

We tend to **look down** on vocational training programs or degrees based on hands-on work. Instead, we chase **prestige.** We want **Master's degrees**, something impressive to brag about. **"My son is studying neuroscience,"** we say with puffed-out chests, as though their accomplishments are somehow **our success.**

Whose Standards Are They, Really?

Some students internalize this pressure more than others. Some parents are more generous, giving their kids freedom to **choose their own path.**

But by the time we're old enough to **gain independence,** many of us are already deeply influenced by our parents' and society's values. And often, we don't even question them.

We think these values are our own, but are they? Without **introspection,** it's hard to know for sure.

Parents Aren't Always Right

Here's a hard truth: your parents don't always know **what's best for you.** They're not always right just because they're your parents.

What they tell you is **"for your own good"** might actually reflect **their own fears,** their **own hopes,** or simply what they were taught themselves.

Most parents genuinely want their kids to be **happy** and **financially secure,** but they often forget that **happiness** means something different to everyone.

For some, happiness is about **exploring the world** or attending **summer camps.** For others, it's about **learning, creating,** or **intellectual stimulation.** And for some, it's about making a **difference** in their community, whether that's a virtual space or the real world.

Your standards might not match your parents', and that's okay.

The Cost of "Never Enough"

Some parents are **hard to please,** no matter how much effort you put in. And let's be honest: the pressure to **"not disappoint"** is exhausting.

When you're constantly chasing approval from parents who always think you could've done better, it takes a toll. Even when you succeed, you're left feeling like it's not **enough.**

This cycle, always striving, never feeling satisfied, can lead to **anxiety** and **low self-esteem.** Worse, it convinces you that **you'll never measure up**. And when you feel like you're not enough for your parents, it's easy to stop feeling like you're enough for yourself.

The Approval You Really Need

Here's the truth: **making your parents proud feels great.** It can boost your confidence when it happens. But constantly chasing that approval, especially if it's impossible to get, can leave you drained and unhappy.

At some point, you have to stop and ask yourself: **Who am I doing this for?**

Between you and me, the **only person** you truly need to make proud is **yourself.** And not through anyone else's eyes, just your own.

TL;DR:

As kids, we seek validation from our parents, often pushing ourselves to meet their expectations. But if we grow up constantly chasing approval from parents who are never satisfied, it can destroy our self-esteem and lead to anxiety. **The only approval you need is your own.** Focus on making **yourself proud**, on your terms, not theirs.

"You Could Have Done Better"

One of the most common beliefs drilled into us is this idea that **we could have done better.** At any moment, in any situation, we're told that if we'd tried harder or been smarter, we would've achieved more.

But what if I told you that, no, you couldn't have?

Let me explain.

Your Brain's Job: Survival

Your **brain** is in charge of everything in your body. Literally **everything.**

It keeps your organs running, processes sensory information, and decides which memories are worth keeping or discarding based on what's relevant to your **survival.** It can even block out traumatic experiences if they're too much to handle.

Your brain doesn't just **store information**—it makes you experience it. The heat of a drink, the sadness of a breakup, the joy of seeing a friend, it's all your brain interpreting **sensory input** and emotional signals based on the **connections it's built over your lifetime.**

Your Brain Always Does Its Best

At any given moment, your brain is operating at the **best capacity it can** given its current state.

- If it's **stressed,** it focuses on protecting you from danger, even if the "danger" is just a tough conversation or a looming deadline.
- If it feels **attacked,** it shifts into defense mode.

Your brain's **only job** is to keep you **alive.** Every decision it makes is based on survival, not perfection.

How Much Control Do We Really Have?

We like to think we're in full control of our brain's processes, but we actually have **less control** than we believe. Sure, we can influence our brain's decisions, but we can't override how it processes information in the moment.

Take this example:

You're sitting in a test and come across a question you don't understand. What can you do?

- The logical solution would be to ask the teacher for clarification, but what if they refuse because it's a test and they think it wouldn't be fair?
- You're stuck with the question, and rereading it over and over doesn't make it any clearer.

You can try breaking it down, finding synonyms, or searching for context clues, but there's a **limit** to what your brain can do. If your brain doesn't understand the question, then **you don't understand it.**

You can't **force** clarity to happen.

The Reality of "Doing Better"

The idea that you could've done better assumes you had **more control** than you actually did. It assumes your brain was holding something back, that it wasn't giving 100%. But that's not how the brain works.

In every moment, your brain is doing the **best it can** with the resources it has, the state it's in, and the situation you're facing.

Sure, you can reflect afterward and think about what could've gone differently, but that doesn't mean you were capable of doing better in the moment.

You weren't lazy, and you didn't fail. You simply reached the **limits** of what your brain could do right then and there. And that's okay.

Another Example: Forgetting During a Test

Picture this: You're sitting in front of your exam, and this time, you understand the question. But the answer? **Gone.** You know you studied it last night, but you just can't remember.

Let me ask you this: Did you forget it on purpose?
Of course not.
Did you decide to forget the information?
No, you didn't.
So how, in that precise moment, could you have **"done better"?**

Maybe you're thinking, **"I could have studied more."** Sure, but that was **yesterday,** not right now.

Or you might tell yourself, **"I could make an effort to remember."** Okay, but how do you actually **force yourself to remember something**? And what if it doesn't work?

The truth is, there's not much you can do. You're already doing your **best** in that exact moment.

Your Best Is Always Relative

The best you can do **right now** is not the same as your best yesterday or tomorrow. It's unique to this very moment, shaped by your **current mental state,** energy, and circumstances.

One of the major flaws of the school system is that it evaluates your understanding of a subject on a **specific day,** at a **specific hour,** with no regard for your **mental state.**

Think about it:

- If you didn't **sleep well** the night before, your memory and focus are likely to suffer.
- If you had a **nightmare** or received **bad news** the day before, your emotions might cloud your ability to concentrate.
- If you're **stressed**, whether from the test itself or life in general, it can impair your ability to **recall information.**

For someone with **ADHD,** these challenges are even more significant. ADHD can impact your **focus, speed,** and **ability to process questions,** and the stress of the test itself can make things even harder.

In that moment, all you can do is your **best** with the mindset and resources you have **right now.**

How many times have you walked out of an exam, and a few hours later, you suddenly **remember the answer** you couldn't recall during the test?

You **knew** the answer, it was there, but the **stress** of the moment blocked your brain's access to it. Once the test was over, the stress lifted, and your memory returned.

It's frustrating, but it's also **completely normal.**

Your Best Depends on the Moment

Your best is a moving target. It's unique to the situation you're in, your energy levels, and your emotional state.

Here's an example:

If I'm exhausted, the best I can do for dinner might be making toast. But if I'm having a great day with plenty of energy, I might spend hours cooking meals for the entire week.

Both are okay. Both are my best at that moment.

We can't demand more from ourselves than what we're capable of in the present moment. **We do what we can, and that's enough.**

The truth is, if you could have **done better** in any given moment, you **would have.** Nobody goes into an exam thinking, **"I'll just leave out the important details on purpose."** We all do our best with the **brain capacity** we have in that moment.

If you're thinking, **"I could've done better if I had studied more"** or **"I shouldn't have procrastinated,"** that's not about the moment itself, that's about how you prepared.

And that's okay. Instead of beating yourself up, use it as an opportunity to **reflect** and **learn** for next time.

The real question isn't, **"Could I have done better?"** but **"What can I do differently next time to get closer to the results I want?"**

TL;DR:

Your "best" changes depending on your energy, mood, stress, and circumstances. Struggling on a test or in any situation doesn't mean you didn't try hard enough, it means that was your best at that moment. Don't dwell on regret; instead, reflect on how you can adjust next time. Remember, your best today might not be your best tomorrow, and that's completely okay.

12

LAZINESS

We can't talk about **capitalism** and **ADHD** without tackling the concept of **laziness.** ADHDers are often called lazy... **very often.** Why? Because **what paralyzes them** is invisible to others.

For neurotypical people, **what seems is what is.** If they see a student scrolling on their phone instead of studying, they assume that person just doesn't **want** to work. They're lazy, plain and simple. This kind of judgment doesn't account for what's happening **inside** that person.

What Is Laziness, Really?

Laziness is typically defined as **"not wanting to work"** or being content with inaction, often with no valid reason. But here's the thing: this definition is **flawed.**

In my opinion, and in the opinion of many therapists and mental health professionals, **laziness doesn't actually exist.** It's not a real thing. It's a **label** created under **capitalism** to shame people for not working.

Remember that under capitalism, your **worth** is tied to your **productivity.** If you're not constantly working or producing something, society labels you as **"lazy."** This isn't by accident. It's a tool used to keep people in line.

Think about it:

- The concept of laziness **guilts you** into constantly working, even at the cost of your mental health. That's why so many of us feel guilty when we take a break.
- The label shifts the blame for **poverty** and **unemployment** onto individuals instead of the system. It's easier to say, **"They're just lazy,"** than to address issues like unequal education, lack of healthcare, or low wages.
- It helps justify the wealth gap. If someone is struggling, it's not because the system is broken; it's because **"they didn't work hard enough."**

By calling people lazy, capitalism ensures that people hustle harder, **fearful** of being judged, while employers get more work for less pay. The result? More wealth flows to the top.

See how messed up that is?
Laziness Isn't Real
In reality, **laziness does not exist.**

It's not a state of being, it's a **judgment.** It's an **opinion** someone forms when they see another person not working, without bothering to ask why.

When someone says, **"They just don't want to work,"** they're oversimplifying a complex situation.

The Bigger Picture
Let's break this down. If someone isn't working, **why?**

- Maybe they have **ADHD** and are paralyzed for reasons we've already discussed—like overwhelm or lack of clarity. They need **understanding and support.**
- Maybe they're **exhausted** or **depressed.**

- Maybe they don't want to work because the task is **boring, repetitive,** and **pointless** to them—especially if they're driven by **intrinsic motivation**, as many ADHDers are.

These are all **valid reasons** for someone to not work. But instead of trying to understand, society defaults to the lazy label.

If we want to truly **help people,** we need to ask, **"What's going on?"** instead of making snap judgments.

TL;DR:

Calling ADHDers "lazy" is common but completely ignores the bigger picture. Laziness is often a label capitalism uses to shame people for not working, tying their worth to productivity. This label shifts blame for poverty and unemployment onto individuals instead of addressing systemic issues like inequality. But laziness isn't real, it's just a judgment made without understanding the reasons behind someone's inaction, whether it's ADHD paralysis, exhaustion, or lack of motivation. Let's stop judging and start asking what's really going on.

Excuse or Reason?

There's a simple but brilliant way someone on the internet once explained the difference between an **excuse** and a **reason**. It goes like this:

An excuse is just a reason that someone considers invalid.

That's it.

When ADHD Is Dismissed as an "Excuse"

So, when someone says, **"Don't take your ADHD as an excuse,"** what they're really saying is that they don't think your **ADHD traits** are valid reasons for your behavior.

Let that sink in.

Your ADHD traits, your challenges with focus, executive functions, time management, are a **core part of how your brain works.** They're not **excuses.** They are valid **reasons** for why you behave the way you do.

Here's the tricky part:

When someone asks, **"What's your excuse?"** they're already framing your explanation as invalid. They're telling you from the start that they won't take you seriously.

But ADHDers need to know this: **Your reasons are valid.** Full stop.

And here's another thing: **"Because I don't want to"** is also a **valid reason** for not doing something.

"I Don't Want To" vs. "I Don't Feel Like It"

There's a subtle but important difference between saying, **"I don't want to"** and **"I don't feel like it."**

- **"I don't want to"** is a firm, categorical **"no."** You do **not** want to do the thing. That's it.

- **"I don't feel like it"** means you'd **rather do something else,** but you might still push yourself to do the thing if it's necessary or important.

This distinction matters. Why? Because while "I don't feel like it" can be a temporary mood, **"I don't want to"** is a boundary.

And both are **valid.**

TL;DR:

An excuse is just a reason someone else doesn't think is valid. When people say, **"Don't use ADHD as an excuse,"** they're dismissing the valid reasons behind your ADHD traits. But your ADHD is a valid reason for your behavior. Also, "I don't want to" is a valid reason for not doing something, and it's different from "I don't feel like it," which means you'd rather do something else. Knowing the difference is important.

13

AGAINST OUR NATURE

First, let's break down what we mean by **"society."** Who or what is it?

In this book, **"society"** refers to **everybody and nobody** at the same time. It's not just individuals, the government, or any specific group. Society is the set of **values, unwritten rules, and beliefs** (not necessarily spiritual) that people collectively agree to live by.

Society is **us,** it's **them,** it's everyone who participates in and perpetuates these shared expectations. It's the **umbrella term** for how a group of people chooses to live, what they believe in, and the rules they follow.

Our Society Today

In **Canada,** where I live, **professional achievements** are highly valued. Success is often measured by your **job title,** how much money you make, or the degree you earned. Even if we don't consciously believe in this system, it's so deeply ingrained in our schools, families, and workplaces that we rarely question it.

It's not just Canada. Many countries, especially in the **Western world,** operate this way. For example, the **United States** shares a similar value system.

But here's the thing: **it's not universal.**

In some countries, the pressure to perform is even worse. Take **Japan**, for example, where heart attack from overwork was so common that they coined a word for it: **karoshi,** which means "death by over-work."

And yet, in other places, it's the opposite. In **Holland,** for instance, the government actively supports its citizens in maintaining a **healthy work-life balance.** On average, Dutch workers put in about **30 hours a week,** compared to Canada's **37.7 hours.**

These are all **developed countries,** yet their approaches to life and work are vastly different.

What We Think Is "Normal"

Because we're used to it, we often assume that the way we live is just **"normal."** We think this is **what it means to live and be human**—that it's this way everywhere, always, and forever.

But that's not true.

What feels **"normal"** to us might be completely **different** elsewhere. And realizing this opens up the possibility of questioning what we've been taught. It challenges us to think about what's actually **natural** for humans and what might actually be **going against our nature.**

You might wonder, **"Why does it even matter?** I still have to live here and deal with this system to get by."

That's true. But **awareness** can be transformative.

When you realize that the way we live is just **one way** of doing things, not the only way, you start to see new possibilities. You can ask yourself:

- **Do I agree with these rules?**
- **Are these values truly my own, or have I just absorbed them from society?**
- **What do I need to feel fulfilled and happy?**

This awareness helps you make **better choices** that align with your own needs and emotions. It creates space for what truly matters to **you.**

Even if we can't change the whole system, we can carve out a life that feels more natural, more aligned, and ultimately, **happier.**

TL;DR:

"Society" refers to the shared values, rules, and beliefs we live by, but these aren't universal. In Canada, for example, professional success is highly valued, but this isn't true everywhere. Some countries, like Japan, overemphasize work, while others, like Holland, prioritize work-life balance. Recognizing that our way of life isn't the only "normal" lets us question what truly matters, understand our own needs, and live in a way that feels more natural and fulfilling, even within the constraints of an imperfect system.

So, What Is Natural for Humans?

When we talk about what's natural for humans, we're not talking about rejecting technology, abandoning modern comforts, or moving back into the woods. It's not about **sexual orientation, identity,** or even the structure of a market-based society.

Instead, it's about understanding the **core needs** and **essence** of human beings—what's universal, no matter where we live or what society we're part of.

The Universal Human Experience

Humans evolve, adapt, and divide into different societies, each with its own culture, rules, and priorities. Today, there are **197 countries** (as of 2024), each shaping its people in unique ways. But here's the key:

No matter the place or culture, humans share the same basic psychological and emotional needs.

When these needs are restricted—such as our **freedom to express emotions, individuality,** or even just our natural tendencies—the result is almost always the same: **unhappiness, frustration, and poor mental health.**

Societies might look different on the outside, but the **essence of human nature** doesn't change.

Humans Are Like Dogs (Hear Me Out)

Let's take dogs as an example. Specifically, let's look at the **husky.**

Huskies were bred to work in cold, snowy environments. They're naturally energetic, hardworking, and enthusiastic about following commands. They were shaped by the needs of the people who raised them: to pull sleds, work in teams, and endure long distances in harsh climates.

Now imagine keeping a husky in a small apartment in Florida, with no exercise, no snow, and no "work" to do. What happens?
It becomes **destructive** and tries to escape. Its natural instincts are being ignored, and it's frustrated.

Humans work the same way.

Neurotypes: The Human Breeds

Just like dog breeds have different characteristics based on where they were bred and for what purpose, **humans have different neurotypes.**

- Some brains, like neurotypical ones, thrive in structured, predictable environments.
- Others, like ADHD or autistic brains, are wired differently, with unique strengths and challenges.

The key difference? Dog breeds were shaped by humans, but **neurotypes either evolved naturally or have existed forever as part of human diversity.**

The Problem With "One-Size-Fits-All" Societies

Imagine forcing a husky to live in Florida without exercise. Or making a bulldog, a dog bred to fight bulls, pull a sled in the Arctic. Neither scenario makes sense because these dogs weren't built for those tasks.

Now imagine forcing an ADHDer or autistic person to function in a society built for neurotypical brains. It's the same thing.

Neurodivergent individuals are **forced to adapt every single day** to a system that wasn't designed for them. This constant adjustment—living against their natural tendencies, takes a massive toll on their mental health and well-being.

Just like a husky needs space to run and a job to do, **neurodivergent people need environments that allow them to thrive.**

What We Can Learn From Dogs

When people adopt a dog, they usually read about the breed—its needs, temperament, and natural instincts. They try to provide an environment that matches the dog's nature because they understand that a happy, well-behaved dog comes from meeting those needs.

We should do the same for humans.

We need to recognize and respect **different neurotypes,** understand what they need, and create spaces where they can thrive—whether that's at home, in schools, or in workplaces.

Because when someone is forced into an environment that goes against their nature, the result is frustration, burnout, and feeling like they don't belong.

TL;DR:

Humans are like different dog breeds, we're all the same species, but our "wiring" is different. ADHDers and autistic people are wired differently from neurotypicals, just like a husky is wired differently from a bulldog. Forcing people with ADHD to function in a neurotypical society is like keeping a husky in a Florida apartment without exercise, it's unnatural, frustrating, and damaging. To thrive, we need environments that match our needs, just like dogs need environments suited to their instincts.

Our School System Works Against ADHD Nature

The North American school system was not designed with ADHD brains in mind, you know that by now. It's structured around **sitting still, following strict schedules,** and focusing on **one thing for long periods.** For someone with ADHD, this setup can feel like an uphill battle every single day.

The system expects **everyone to learn the same way, at the same pace,** and in the same environment. But ADHD brains aren't wired for monotony. As we stated before, they thrive on **creativity, movement, and variety,** not on repetitive tasks or rigid routines.

Why It Feels Like a Struggle

Schools tend to emphasize **memorization, standardized tests,** and sticking to **strict routines.** These methods prioritize conformity over individuality, leaving little room for students with ADHD to express their unique strengths.

And ADHDers *do* have strengths: **quick thinking, creativity, and innovative problem-solving.** But these traits often go unnoticed or undervalued because they don't fit the mold of what schools define as success.

Instead of feeling celebrated for these gifts, students with ADHD are often made to feel like they're constantly **falling behind.**

It's Not About Being "Not Smart Enough"

When the system doesn't recognize or support how your brain works, it's easy to feel:

- **Frustrated:** Why can't I focus like everyone else?

- **Bored:** Why does this feel so dull?
- **Inadequate:** Why am I not smart enough?

The truth is, **you are smart enough.** The problem isn't your brain, it's the system trying to force everyone into the same mold. ADHD brains were **never built** to thrive in an environment that values sitting still and doing the same tasks over and over. Which doesn't mean that ADHDers cannot succeed at school! But knowing they are in an environment that goes against their nature, they can adapt and find systems to help, instead of fighting themselves into functioning like a neutorypical student.

What ADHD Brains Need

To truly shine, ADHD students need environments that encourage:

- **Movement:** Instead of sitting still for hours, let's incorporate hands-on learning.
- **Variety:** Mix up teaching methods to keep things fresh and engaging.
- **Creative Thinking:** Allow students to explore ideas from different angles rather than focusing solely on rote memorization.

When these needs are met, ADHD students don't just keep up, they excel! They bring fresh ideas, unique perspectives, and boundless creativity to the table.

TL;DR:

The North American school system isn't designed for ADHD brains. It expects everyone to sit still, follow strict schedules, and focus on repetitive tasks—all things that ADHDers struggle with. ADHD minds thrive on creativity, movement, and variety, but the current system often makes these students feel like they're falling behind or not smart enough. The problem isn't you—it's the system not recognizing your strengths.

Our Society Is Based on an Illusion

The pressures we feel (finishing school quickly, landing a "good job," making the elusive "6 figures") are not universal truths. **They're illusions.** They're products of societal brainwashing, so ingrained in our everyday lives that they feel like reality. But they're not.

If you've ever questioned these beliefs, you might have noticed how strongly people react. That's because they've been taught, just like you, that these ideas are the way life *has* to be. But when you look at different cultures, you start to realize something important: **what's "normal" here isn't normal everywhere.**

The Ham Story

Let me tell you a little story to explain:

Once, there was a family who, every winter holiday, made ham for dinner. The father always cut the ham in half, putting each piece into a separate dish before seasoning and cooking it.

One day, his young daughter asked, **"Daddy, why do you cut the ham in half?"**

The father replied, **"That's the way my mom always made it, and her ham was always delicious!"**

Curious, the little girl went to her grandmother and asked, **"Grandma, why do you cut the ham in half?"**

The grandmother replied, **"That's the way my father always made it. His ham was perfect!"**

Finally, the girl asked her great-grandfather, **"Papi, why do you cut the ham in half?"**

He laughed and said, **"Oh, sweetheart, I only did that because I didn't have a dish big enough to cook the whole ham!"**

This story teaches us something important: **many "rules" we follow today once had valid reasons, but those reasons may no longer apply.**

How Societal Norms Change

Take **smoking** as an example.

In the 1960s, smoking was encouraged. It was glamorized in TV ads, and few people knew the health risks (besides the tobacco industry, but that's another story). Up until the 1990s, it was still acceptable to smoke in schools and hospitals! But as society learned more about its dangers, things changed. Smoking is now heavily regulated and discouraged for the sake of public health.

The same is true for **baby care, food recommendations, and road safety.** Practices change over time as we gain new information. What was once "normal" can turn out to be harmful, and society adjusts to protect people.

Why We Struggle With Change

Humans crave **stability** and familiarity. We like our routines, our rules, and the idea that "this is just the way it is." Changing those rules, especially ones that have been around for a long time, can feel deeply unsettling.

This is why some people fight against change, sometimes for decades or even forever. It's not because they're bad people; it's because change feels like stepping into the unknown, and that's scary.

What This Means For Us

The norms we live by, like the rush to get a good job or earn a high salary, aren't universal truths. They're just **one version of reality** that our society has decided to adopt. Other cultures prioritize different things, like family, community, or happiness.

Understanding this is freeing. Once you realize these pressures are just constructs, you can start to question them:

- **Do I really need to rush through school, or can I go at my own pace?**
- **Does my job define my worth, or is there more to who I am?**
- **Am I chasing goals that truly matter to me, or just ones society says I should care about?**

Questioning the system doesn't mean rejecting it entirely, it means giving yourself the freedom to decide what actually matters to you.

TL;DR:

The pressure to finish school fast, get a "good job," or make "6 figures" is an illusion. These ideas aren't universal truths—they're societal norms we've been taught. Different cultures prioritize different things, proving there's no one "right" way to live. Just like outdated rules about smoking or baby care, what seems normal now might not actually be good for us. Questioning these norms helps us live more authentically, even if change feels uncomfortable at first.

But What About Our Psychological Health?

For how long have we been living in ways that hurt our mental health, without really addressing the root of the problem? We keep funding mental health services and creating more resources, which is good, but we're not doing nearly enough to prevent these issues from happening in the first place. As someone close to me once said, **"It's important to help people who are struggling, but we should focus more on preventing the struggle from starting at all."**

The Problem With Old Norms

Just because a set of values or rules feels **"set in stone"** doesn't mean it's the only way to live. Sure, some people find meaning in these traditional values, but for many others, they're suffocating and **don't align with who we are.**

When we try to live by outdated norms, it's like forcing ourselves into a mold that doesn't fit. Over time, this pressure can seriously mess with our mental health. Here's why:

- **It creates constant stress:** Trying to meet unrealistic expectations can leave us feeling like we're never enough.
- **It damages self-esteem:** When we don't fit the mold, we blame ourselves for not measuring up, even though the problem isn't us, it's the mold.
- **It ignores diversity:** These old norms often fail to account for different neurotypes, personal struggles, or unique needs, leaving many without the support they deserve.

When The Rules Don't Match Who You Are

Imagine living in a world where you're forced to follow rules that clash with your natural way of being. For ADHDers, for example, society's emphasis on rigid schedules, productivity, and strict standards doesn't fit how their brains work.

When the **rules don't align with your true self,** it leads to frustration, burnout, and even isolation. It's not just about feeling out of place, it's about constantly being told, directly or indirectly, that who you are isn't "right."

The consequences go beyond individuals. A society stuck in outdated values can't grow or improve, leaving everyone behind, not just those who feel out of place. If we want a healthier, more inclusive future, we need to question these norms, **challenge the status quo,** and push for changes that prioritize mental and emotional well-being.

Change Won't Be Instant—But It's Necessary

No, you can't change the laws or completely rewrite society on your own. But **awareness is powerful.** The more we question what we've been taught and understand how these norms affect us, the more likely we are to demand change. Not just for ourselves but for future generations.

At the end of the day, society should support us, not break us down. To do that, we need to let go of the "one-size-fits-all" approach and focus on systems that **actually nurture human well-being.**

TL;DR:

We're spending loads on mental health services but ignoring the root cause: the outdated norms and rules that stress people out. Living by these old values can hurt self-esteem, create constant stress, and fail to account for diversity, like different neurotypes. To truly support mental health, we need to question these norms and push for change that prioritizes well-being. Even if we can't change society overnight, recognizing the problem is the first step toward progress.

14

DEBUNKING MYTHS

"Job of a Lifetime"

At 17, it feels like the world is pressuring you to pick the **perfect career path,** one that will define the rest of your life. But here's the thing: **it doesn't have to.**

Think about it. Could you, 10 years ago, have made the perfect choice for who you are today? Maybe, but most likely not. That's because we **change a lot** over time: our interests, our goals, even the people we surround ourselves with. At 17, your brain isn't even fully developed yet (that won't happen until around age 25), and yet you're expected to make a decision that will supposedly last a lifetime.

The Truth About Career Choices

A career path you pick at 17 or 18 will **probably not** be the one you stick with forever. And that's perfectly okay. It's just your **starting point.** Your first job, your first degree, or your first training program isn't a life sentence, it's an opportunity to explore and figure out what works for you *right now.*

Don't Try to Predict the Future

It's natural to worry about the long term. You might think, **"But I don't want to change careers or go back to school when I'm older!"** And that's a valid concern. But here's the reality: you **can't know for sure** what future-you will want. The person you are at 30 might have completely different interests, priorities, and passions than the person you are now.

So, instead of stressing about picking the "perfect" career for a version of yourself you haven't even met yet, focus on what feels right for the **present you.** Let future-you figure out their own path when the time comes.

It's Okay to Change

Some people stick with the same career their whole lives, and that's fine if it works for them. But for many, shifting careers or going back to school later on is part of their journey. If you're open to change, you're giving yourself the flexibility to adapt, grow, and pursue new opportunities as they come.

What matters now is making a choice that aligns with **who you are today.** Not the person you'll be in 10 or 20 years, but the person sitting here reading this.

TL;DR:

Choosing a career at 17 doesn't mean you're locked into it for life. Your brain and interests will change a lot in the next decade, so your first career is just your **starting point.** Don't stress about future-you; make the best choice for who you are **right now.** Let future-you handle the rest, and remember—it's okay to change paths if you need to.

Do You Really Need a Six-Figure Salary?

It's true that since the 2020 pandemic, life has become more expensive. We need a certain amount of money to live without financial stress. But here's the thing: how much money you actually need depends heavily on your **lifestyle choices.**

Do you prefer a small apartment or a house?
Do you use public transport or own a car (or two)?
Do you cook most meals at home, or do you eat out often?
Do you prioritize travel, or are you more of a homebody?

What Really Matters?

The key is understanding what truly brings you joy. Society often pushes the idea that **more money equals more happiness,** but the reality is more nuanced. If you align your spending with your actual priorities, you may find you don't need as much as you thought.

For example, if you love simplicity, like living in a cozy apartment, using public transportation, and cooking at home, your financial needs are much lower than someone chasing a lifestyle of large homes, multiple cars, and constant dining out. It's all about **what feels right for you.**

The Power of a Budget

Here's an important point: financial freedom isn't about making endless amounts of money, it's about learning to **manage what you already have.** A budget isn't just for people who are broke or struggling; it's a tool that can help anyone reduce financial stress and live with more control.

When we hear "budget," it often feels negative, like it means cutting out all the fun stuff. But really, budgeting is about **choosing what matters.** It's not about deprivation, it's about directing your money toward the things you value most.

For example, you might skip a $5 coffee every morning so you can afford a weekend getaway. Or you might spend less on dining out so you can splurge on a hobby you love. **A budget gives you control, and with control comes peace of mind.**

The Myth of Instant Six-Figure Success

Here's the reality: most people don't start their careers earning a six-figure salary. It often takes **years of work and experience** to reach that level, and that's completely normal. Thinking you need to hit that number right away, or even ever, is setting yourself up for unnecessary pressure.

Besides, focusing solely on a high income can backfire. Many people earn six figures yet feel trapped in stressful, unfulfilling jobs. Money alone doesn't guarantee happiness, especially if you've sacrificed your mental health or values to get it.

Your Path, Your Pace

The goal isn't to earn a specific salary, it's to build a life that aligns with your values. Maybe you want the flexibility to work fewer hours so you can enjoy time with loved ones. Maybe you're okay with a smaller apartment if it means you can spend more on travel. Whatever it is, **define success on your own terms.**

And remember, financial freedom often comes from **smart management** of your resources, not necessarily a massive paycheck. You might find that with the right budget and priorities, you're already closer to freedom than you think.

TL;DR:

How much money you need to live stress-free depends on your lifestyle. A six-figure salary isn't necessary if you align your spending with your values and manage your finances well. Budgeting isn't about cutting out fun—it's about taking control and prioritizing what matters to you. Most people don't start out earning six figures anyway, so don't stress about chasing a number. Focus on creating a life that works for **you.**

You're Just Not Making Enough Effort

Ah yes, the ultimate ADHD myth: "You just need to make more effort." Let's unpack this, but first, let's try a quick exercise.

Define "effort" in a way that leaves no room for interpretation. Go ahead, take a moment.

...

...

Stuck? That's because "effort" is ridiculously subjective.

The dictionary defines effort as a "vigorous or determined attempt," with "vigorous" meaning "strong, healthy, and full of energy." But how does that translate to real life? For one person, effort might mean **powering through a tough task until it's done.** For someone else, it could mean **trying again after failing.** For another, it's **breaking the task into smaller pieces just to get started.**

Now, let's think about how this applies to ADHD. If we're already working against executive functioning differences, difficulty with planning, focus, prioritization, memory, or task initiation—what does "just try harder" even mean?

Effort Isn't the Point

The thing is, ADHD isn't about **not trying hard enough.** It's not about being lazy, careless, or indifferent. ADHD is about real, measurable differences in how the brain is wired, specifically in executive functions. These differences affect how we process information, manage tasks, and respond to challenges.

Telling someone with ADHD to "make more effort" completely ignores how executive functions actually work. It's like asking someone with poor eyesight to "squint harder" to see better. Sure, they could squint, but what they really need is **glasses**—a tool that accommodates their difference.

In the same way, ADHD isn't about needing to "care more" or "push harder." It's about **learning strategies, using tools, and creating systems** to work with your brain instead of against it. These accommodations don't magically make the disability disappear, they help bypass some of the challenges, but the underlying differences in how our brains work will always be there.

What Effort Really Looks Like

For an ADHDer, effort can look very different from how it looks for a neurotypical person. It might be:

- **Writing a to-do list** because keeping track of everything mentally is impossible.
- **Setting timers** to remind yourself to move to the next task.
- **Asking for help** when a task feels overwhelming.
- **Starting and stopping a task 15 times** because sticking with it for long stretches is hard.

These things might not look like "effort" to someone else, but for ADHD brains, they can take a monumental amount of energy.

And here's the kicker: even with all that effort, it doesn't always lead to success or progress. Again, that's because ADHD isn't about "not trying hard enough", it's about the brain being wired differently.

The Harm in "Just Try Harder"

Telling someone with ADHD that they just need to try harder is not only unhelpful, but it's also harmful. It invalidates their experiences and the real struggles they face every day. Worse, it perpetuates a cycle of shame:

- **"I'm failing because I'm not trying hard enough."**
- **"I'm clearly not good enough."**
- **"Why can't I just do this like everyone else?"**

This isn't just untrue, it's toxic.

Instead of focusing on effort, we need to shift the conversation toward **understanding, support, and accommodations.** ADHD brains aren't broken; they just operate differently. Recognizing this difference is the first step toward finding solutions that work.

TL;DR:

A big myth about ADHD is that we just need to "try harder." But what does "effort" even mean? It's subjective and doesn't take into account the executive functioning differences at the core of ADHD. ADHD isn't about being lazy or not caring—it's about a brain wired differently. Managing ADHD means creating systems and accommodations to bypass challenges, not trying to force the brain to work like a neurotypical one. So no, we're not "not trying enough"—we're just working within a totally different framework.

If You're Not Set by 25, You're Late

Let's start with the obvious: expecting to have your life completely figured out by **25** is *ridiculous.*

Here's a fun fact: the whole "be settled by 25" milestone was set *hundreds of years ago,* when the average human lifespan was about 50. It hasn't been updated to match today's reality. Back then, you had to cram a lot of life into fewer years. But today? That timeline makes zero sense.

Think about it. By the age of **25, your brain has only just finished maturing.** You're literally still growing into yourself. Today, most people don't settle into their careers or lives until their **30s or even later.** Expecting someone to "have it all" by 25 is outdated and harmful. It puts ridiculous pressure on young adults trying to find their way.

But I Don't Want to Wait Until 30!

Totally valid. When you're in your late teens or early 20s, you crave independence and freedom. You want to figure out who you are, what you want, and where you're going. And some people do manage to get settled by 25, more power to them!

The problem isn't striving for it; the problem is *expecting it from everyone.* When society pushes this milestone as some universal rule, it creates stress, self-doubt, and comparison.

Life Isn't a Straight Line

Here's the reality: **life isn't a race or a checklist.** It's a winding road full of unexpected detours, dead ends, and surprising new paths. Some people figure things out early, but many take their time. And both are **totally valid.**

The pressure to "have it all" by 25 makes you feel like you're behind before you've even really started. But you're not behind. **You're just living.**

Instead of rushing to meet some arbitrary deadline, focus on exploring who you are. Your 20s are a time to experiment, grow, and figure out what makes you happy. Try new things. Make mistakes. Learn from them. It's not about ticking off a list, it's about creating a life that feels meaningful *to you*.

The "Tutorial" Phase of Life

Here's an analogy for my fellow geeks: think of the first **18 years** of life as the tutorial phase of a video game. You're learning the controls, figuring out the rules, and testing what works.

When you hit 18 or 20, the real game begins. You're level **1**—not **25**. You're not supposed to "beat the game" by 25 years old, but some people like to speedrun. And that's fine! But for most of us, life is about playing at your own pace, leveling up when you're ready, and enjoying the adventure.

Success Has No Deadline

At the end of the day, **success doesn't have an expiration date.** Some people find their calling at 22. Others at 42. It's all about finding a path that works for you, not rushing to fit into someone else's timeline.

So, take a deep breath. **There's no rush.** Life isn't about having it all figured out, it's about growing, changing, and building a life that feels true to who you are.

TL;DR:

The idea that you need your life set by 25 is outdated and unrealistic. It comes from a time when people didn't live as long, and it doesn't fit today's reality. Your brain isn't even fully mature until 25, and most people settle down closer to their 30s.

Life isn't a straight line or a race, it's a winding road where everyone moves at their own pace. Focus on exploring, growing, and figuring out what makes you happy, instead of chasing arbitrary deadlines. Success doesn't have a timeline, so enjoy the journey instead of stressing about the destination.

BEING A STUDENT WITH ADHD

THE SCHOOL SYSTEM

H ere we are, diving into the main topic now that we've laid the groundwork

The school system

Schools have been around in one form or another for thousands of years. In ancient times, think Egypt, Greece, or China, education was mainly reserved for the upper class, grooming future leaders, priests, and scribes. These early schools taught religious texts, philosophy, and administrative skills.

Fast forward to the **19th century** and the Industrial Revolution. Societies became more industrialized, which meant they needed educated and skilled workers to fill jobs in factories and offices. This is when the idea of **mandatory public education** began. Schools were created to teach all kids, not just the wealthy, the basics: reading, writing, math, and skills to work in an industrialized world.

By the **20th century**, schools expanded beyond the basics to prepare students for a growing variety of jobs. Education systems were restructured to ensure students could meet the demands of an economy that was becoming more specialized.

If early schools were designed to create **thinkers**, modern schools evolved to produce **workers.** And that's fine to a certain extent, many people thrive in traditional work roles.

Neurotypes and Society: A Theory

There's an interesting theory about how different neurotypes align with roles in society:

- **Neurotypical people are the workers.** They often excel in traditional roles, take pride in their contributions, and thrive in structured environments like companies or organizations.
- **ADHDers are the inventors and creators.** Their strengths lie in innovation, creative problem-solving, and coming up with big ideas that break the mold. They shine in roles that value these qualities.
- **Autistic people are the thinkers.** They excel in roles requiring deep focus, analysis, and insight. Their satisfaction often comes from understanding complex systems and ideas.

This doesn't mean neurotypical folks can't invent, or that ADHDers and autistic people can't work traditional jobs. It's more about what each neurotype often **thrives** in and where they find fulfillment.

What Modern Schools Actually Teach

Here's the issue: modern schools are structured to produce **workers**, not **inventors** or **thinkers.** And if the system is built to make workers, it's easy to see why neurodivergent people struggle. They're not being nurtured for their natural strengths.

Schools don't just teach math, history, or science. They teach **routine**.

- You go to school from **8 to 4** every day, just like a **9-to-5 workday**.
- You're taught to follow schedules, be on time, and stick to structure. These are all traits that are essential in traditional jobs.

For neurotypical students, this system often works well because their brains naturally adapt to structured routines. They're being prepared to seamlessly transition into a workforce that values punctuality, consistency, and adherence to routine.

For ADHDers and autistic students, this rigidity can feel suffocating. Their brains thrive on **creativity**, **curiosity**, or **focused analysis**, but the current school structure rarely allows for that. Instead, they're constantly told to fit into a mold that wasn't designed for them.

A One-Size-Fits-All Model

The problem is that the school system assumes everyone learns the same way, at the same pace, in the same environment. But this one-size-fits-all approach doesn't work for **every brain.**

It prioritizes:

- **Memorization** over creativity.
- **Standardized tests** over unique problem-solving approaches.
- **Conformity** over individual strengths.

This system measures success in very narrow terms, leaving many neurodivergent students feeling like they're failing, not because they're not capable, but because the system wasn't built with them in mind.

Why This Matters

Education is supposed to nurture a person's potential, but for many neurodivergent students, it does the opposite. Instead of helping them flourish, the system:

- **Dismisses their strengths.** Creativity, curiosity, and deep thinking aren't prioritized.
- **Highlights their struggles.** ADHDers may be called out for not sitting still, and autistic students may feel overwhelmed by social and sensory demands.

- **Forces them to adapt.** Neurodivergent students have to spend their energy trying to fit into the system, rather than using it to excel at what they're naturally good at.

The school system doesn't just teach you subjects, it teaches you how to live in a society that values **routine, structure, and productivity** above all else. For those whose brains work differently, this creates a constant struggle to feel "good enough."

The Bigger Picture

Schools play a massive role in shaping who we become and how we see ourselves. When a system isn't built to support your strengths or meet your needs, it can leave you feeling like you're failing. But the truth is, it's not you—it's the system.

We need to rethink how we approach education to make room for **all kinds of brains.** A more inclusive system would recognize that inventors, thinkers, and workers all have unique roles to play in society. By nurturing each neurotype's strengths instead of forcing them into a rigid mold, we can create a world where everyone thrives.

Homework and the Worker Mentality

Let's be real: **homework** is like unpaid overtime. On the surface, it's supposed to help students practice what they've learned, but in reality, it's teaching them something deeper: putting in **extra time and effort** beyond what's required, something employers love to see.

It's not just about academics. Homework is a **hidden lesson** in becoming the ideal worker:

- It **rewards productivity**, deadlines, and consistency.
- It **normalizes authority**, teaching students to follow rules, even when they have their own (possibly better) ways of doing things.
- It **reflects capitalism**, where time is money, and where working after hours (without breaks!) is often glorified.

And then there's the **race for grades**, which mirrors the adult race for promotions, better jobs, and higher salaries. It's not just about learning anymore, it's about **competing.**

Why Study Tips Don't Always Work

Throughout their school years, ADHD students are bombarded with **study tips** that were designed by and for neurotypical people:

- "Use flashcards!"
- "Stick to a study schedule!"
- "Eliminate all distractions!"

Some of these tips might help a little, but most don't align with how ADHD brains operate. Instead of realizing the mismatch, ADHD students often **blame themselves** for not being able to stick to these methods. They think, *"I must be the problem."*

The Impact of Being Undiagnosed

Many ADHD students go through their entire education **undiagnosed**, which makes things even worse. While diagnosed ADHD students might at least know they have "trouble focusing" or struggle with executive functions, undiagnosed students are left completely in the dark.

They don't understand *why* they can't keep up with their classmates. They assume they're just **bad students** or not as smart as everyone else. This takes a huge toll on their **self-esteem**, often leading to feelings of inadequacy and even hopelessness.

The School System Isn't Changing Anytime Soon

Unfortunately, **alternative schools**—which often cater better to neurodivergent students—are rare and hard to get into. The majority of students, neurotypical and neurodivergent alike, are stuck in a system that hasn't evolved much since it was designed to churn out factory workers during the Industrial Revolution.

For ADHD students, this means spending their formative years in an environment that doesn't align with their strengths, making them feel like they're always falling short. It's **not because they're incapable**, but because the system wasn't built for their brains.

A System in Need of Change

The current school system may teach discipline, routine, and productivity, but it fails to nurture **creativity, curiosity, and adaptability**—qualities that ADHD students have in abundance. If schools were designed to embrace these traits, ADHD students wouldn't just survive; they'd thrive.

But until real changes happen, it's crucial for ADHD students (and their parents) to recognize that the **problem isn't them**. It's the system. They are not broken; they're just navigating a structure that wasn't built for their incredible, creative, and dynamic brains.

TL;DR

Homework mirrors unpaid overtime, and schools are more about creating workers than nurturing creativity. The rigid, standardized system works for neurotypical students but clashes with ADHD brains, which thrive on freedom, curiosity, and variety.

Most study tips and school strategies are designed for neurotypical learners, leaving ADHD students feeling like they're the problem when the real issue is the system itself. Undiagnosed ADHD students often struggle the most, blaming themselves for their difficulties.

The school system isn't changing anytime soon, but understanding that ADHD students *aren't the problem* is the first step toward supporting them in a system that wasn't built for their strengths.

THE PRIVILEGE OF DIAGNOSIS

The Privilege of Diagnosis
Let's pause for a moment to talk about something crucial: **the privilege of being diagnosed.**

As we've touched on before, **many people don't fully understand what ADHD is.** They think it's just about trouble paying attention, and because of that narrow view, a huge number of ADHDers remain **undiagnosed.**

If a student does well in school? Forget it. No one's going to ask questions about how they're coping internally. After all, society tends to assume that **grades = success.** If they're acing their classes, then clearly, everything's fine, right? (Spoiler: *it's not.*)

A Diagnosis Isn't Guaranteed

Here's the harsh truth: only a **tiny portion** of ADHDers ever get a diagnosis. Why? There are two big reasons:

1. **Access to professionals is limited.** Finding a licensed professional to diagnose ADHD can be like finding a needle in a haystack, especially in areas with long waitlists or limited healthcare resources.

2. **The cost is high.** ADHD assessments can cost anywhere from **a few hundred to $1,500 or more.** For many families, that's simply not affordable, especially if insurance doesn't cover the testing.

This creates a massive **privilege gap.** Those who are diagnosed are often the ones who have the financial means, the right support systems, or live in places with accessible mental health services. Meanwhile, countless others go through life undiagnosed, struggling silently, often blaming themselves for their difficulties.

Undiagnosed ADHD's Hidden Toll

Without a diagnosis, ADHDers don't have access to accommodations, tools, or even the **validation** that comes with understanding why their brain works the way it does. They might spend years feeling:

- **Frustrated**, because they can't figure out why they're struggling.
- **Ashamed**, because they think they're lazy or broken.
- **Exhausted**, from constantly masking and trying to keep up with neurotypical expectations.

A diagnosis can be life-changing. It's not just about getting formal accommodations (though that's a big part of it), it's about finally **seeing the full picture** of who you are and why certain things feel so much harder than they "should."

The fact that a diagnosis is often tied to **wealth and privilege** is yet another way our current systems fail neurodivergent people.

Depending on where you live, there might be **free autism assessments** available (especially in certain schools or public health systems). But ADHD? **Good luck.** ADHD assessments are almost always **privately funded,** and I'm still waiting to hear about a free one.

This creates yet another barrier for ADHDers, especially students who might desperately need help but can't get it because their families can't afford the expensive diagnostic process.

Diagnosis as a Gatekeeper

Many schools insist that students have an **official diagnosis** in order to access **accommodations.**

Let's pause and think about that.

If a student is struggling, whether it's with focus, time management, emotional regulation, or simply trying to sit still long enough to complete an assignment, **why should they need a diagnosis to get help?**

Struggling is struggling.

Why does it matter if it's ADHD, autism, or something else?

The purpose of accommodations is to give students the support they need to thrive in the system. Requiring a formal diagnosis before offering that support is **backward**. It punishes students for being in a position where they can't afford help in the first place.

A System Stacked Against ADHDers

Here's the reality: the students who need the most help often get the least support. Those without diagnoses are left to struggle, their challenges dismissed or misinterpreted as laziness, defiance, or "not trying hard enough." And even when schools do acknowledge the need for accommodations, they often say, **"Well, we can't do anything until you have a diagnosis."**

This approach ignores the fundamental issue: students with ADHD (or other struggles) don't need a label to deserve help. They just need someone to notice their difficulties and step in with **compassion** and **practical solutions.**

Imagine if schools took the stance that **any student who struggles deserves help, period.** No hoops to jump through. No expensive assessments required. Just **support based on the actual needs of the child.**

But that would require a shift in how we view education and its purpose—not to mention a huge overhaul of funding and resource allocation.

TL;DR

Even if you believe in ADHD, most people can't afford a diagnosis, and free assessments are extremely rare. Schools often insist on having a diagnosis to offer accommodations, but this punishes struggling students who can't get one. Struggling should be enough to get help—whether there's a diagnosis or not. Accommodations shouldn't be gatekept behind an expensive process. Students deserve support based on their needs, not their access to healthcare.

17

THE ROLE OF TEACHERS

The Role of Teachers

Teachers aren't just there to lecture and hand out assignments. Their job is to make sure **every student understands the material**—and that means adjusting their teaching styles to suit different learning needs. **Everyone learns differently**, whether they're neurotypical or neurodivergent, and teaching should reflect that diversity.

Individual Support Matters

To see if a student is struggling, don't just ask the class, **"Does everyone understand?"** Most students won't raise their hands, either because they're afraid of being judged or don't want to slow things down. Instead, teachers should take the time to check in with students **individually.** A quick one-on-one conversation can uncover what a student isn't grasping and offer them the opportunity to ask for help without the pressure of an audience.

Celebrating Neurodiversity

Teachers play a **huge role in fostering inclusion** and celebrating neurodiversity in schools. By understanding that each student **thinks and learns in their own way,** they can adapt their methods to help everyone shine. For example:

- A student with **ADHD** might thrive in creative tasks or problem-solving activities.
- An **autistic student** might excel in precision and attention to detail.

Recognizing these differences isn't about giving anyone special treatment; it's about **leveling the playing field** so every student has the chance to succeed. It's about moving beyond grades to see and appreciate the **unique strengths** each student brings to the classroom.

Making Learning Inclusive

When teachers **embrace neurodiversity**, they create an environment where everyone benefits. Adapting lessons to showcase students' strengths not only helps individual growth but also enriches the learning experience for the entire class.

Think of a classroom where creativity, problem-solving, analytical thinking, and attention to detail are all valued equally. Students learn to appreciate each other's talents and collaborate more effectively. And when teachers encourage this kind of inclusive learning, they equip students with skills that go beyond academics, like empathy, adaptability, and teamwork.

TL;DR
Teachers do more than teach, they're crucial to creating inclusive learning environments. By checking in with students individually and adapting their methods, they can support different learning styles. Celebrating neurodiversity makes the classroom stronger: students with ADHD might excel in creativity and problem-solving, while autistic students might shine in detailed work. When teachers focus on these strengths, they help students grow and enrich the learning experience for everyone.

18

UNDERSTANDING STRESS

Understanding Stress
Stress is an **automatic response of the brain** to a perceived threat. It's not inherently bad, in fact, stress has been key to our survival as a species. But when unmanaged or misunderstood, it can negatively impact things like studies, work, or overall well-being.

What is Stress?

Stress is your brain's **alarm system**, kicking into high gear when it senses danger. Think of it as your survival instinct taking over. Here's a scenario to illustrate:

Imagine it's thousands of years ago. You're peacefully tending to your crops while your kids play nearby. Someone is cooking a meal, and everything is calm. Suddenly, a tiger appears.

Your brain immediately detects the threat. Everything you were doing, whether it's chores, eating, or playing, gets pushed aside. All your brain cares about now is **survival.**

You'll either:

- **Fight** the tiger, or
- **Flee** and find safety.

This is the **fight-or-flight response,** and it's driven by stress.

Why This Matters Today

While tigers aren't a daily threat anymore, your brain still reacts to **modern stressors** the same way it would to a tiger. The threat might not be life-threatening: it could be a big exam, an overwhelming to-do list, or a conflict with someone. But your brain doesn't know the difference; it treats all stressors like survival-level dangers.

The problem is that the **fight-or-flight response** wasn't designed to last for long periods. When stress becomes chronic, meaning it sticks around for weeks, months, or years, it starts taking a toll on your mental and physical health.

Understanding stress isn't about avoiding it completely (which is impossible). Instead, it's about **managing it** so it doesn't control your life.

Stay tuned! We'll explore how stress affects learning and focus, and what you can do to reduce its impact.

Stress Factors

Stress kicks in when your brain senses a **threat**, even if it's not life-threatening. Understanding what triggers stress can help you manage it better. There are **four main factors** that your brain registers as stressful:

1. Poor Control

Not having control over a situation can be one of the most stressful experiences. When you feel powerless to change or influence what's happening, your brain interprets it as a threat, leading to heightened stress and anxiety.

Think about waiting for the results of a job interview or dealing with an unexpected accident. You can't control the outcome, and that helplessness keeps your brain in constant alert mode.

2. Unpredictability

Your brain *loves* predictability. It craves knowing what's coming next so it can feel secure. When things are uncertain or up in the air, your brain gets uncomfortable and perceives the unknown as a potential danger. This creates a lot of stress because your brain can't plan or prepare.

Picture walking into a job interview. You don't know who you'll meet, what questions they'll ask, or how it'll go. This unpredictability spikes stress levels, even if the situation itself isn't dangerous.

3. Novelty

New or unfamiliar situations can be exciting, but they're also a **stress trigger**. Your brain doesn't have prior experiences to guide it, so it treats novelty with caution. This "better safe than sorry" response puts your brain on high alert, just in case the new thing turns out to be dangerous.

For example, starting a new job or moving to a new city is a fresh experience, but it can feel overwhelming because your brain hasn't adjusted yet. Even positive changes can carry a layer of stress.

4. Threat to the Ego

This is one of the sneakiest stress triggers. When your self-image or abilities feel challenged, it hits at your core. Whether it's public speaking, receiving criticism, or feeling like you're failing, these situations can shake your confidence and spike your stress levels.

Think of having to do a school presentation in front of your class. You're exposed, open to judgment, and terrified that your flaws might be on display. It's not just about the task, it's about how it affects your sense of self-worth.

Why This Matters

Recognizing these stress factors (poor control, unpredictability, novelty, and ego threats) helps you understand why certain situations make you feel the way you do. Once you know what's triggering your stress, you can start taking steps to **manage** it, whether that's by preparing more for unpredictable events, focusing on what you *can* control, or building your confidence to handle ego threats.

TL;DR

Stress is your brain's natural reaction to anything it sees as a threat. Four key triggers are:

1. **Poor Control**: Feeling powerless over a situation.
2. **Unpredictability**: Not knowing what's coming next.
3. **Novelty**: Facing new or unfamiliar experiences.
4. **Threat to Ego**: Situations that challenge your self-image or confidence.

Understanding these stress factors can help you identify your triggers and take steps to manage them effectively.

What Does Stress Do to Your Body and Brain?

Stress is your body's **emergency survival mode**. It's all about helping you handle danger, whether it's real or perceived. When you're stressed, your brain flips the switch on a series of physical and mental changes to focus entirely on survival.

Adrenaline Surge

The moment your brain senses a threat, it releases stress hormones like **adrenaline**. This gives you a sudden burst of energy, making you super alert, fast, and strong. Your body is gearing up for a classic **"fight or flight"** response.

Heart Rate and Blood Flow

Your heart starts beating harder and faster, sending extra **blood and oxygen** to your muscles. Why? Because your body is preparing you to either run like crazy or stand and fight. This also means that less energy is going toward things like thinking or remembering, as those aren't essential for immediate survival.

Digestion Slows Down

When you're in stress mode, your body assumes escaping danger is more important than breaking down lunch. So, **digestion takes a backseat**. All the energy usually used for processing food is rerouted to your muscles and brain to keep you alert and ready to act.

Pause on Long-Term Thinking

Deep thinking, problem-solving, and memory are put on hold. Stress doesn't care about your exam tomorrow or the big presentation next week. Your brain is focused on **now**, not later.

Why Does This Happen?

Your body is wired to **protect you from danger**, whether it's a literal tiger chasing you (like in prehistoric times) or a metaphorical one, like a looming deadline or a difficult conversation. This response made sense when survival meant outrunning predators, but in today's world, your brain reacts the same way to non-life-threatening stressors, like a school test or a packed schedule.

The Catch?

Stress is helpful in short bursts; it can save your life or help you power through a tough situation. But if you're stressed all the time, this constant survival mode can wear you out physically and mentally, leading to problems like burnout, anxiety, and even health issues.

TL;DR

Stress activates your body's **survival mode**, releasing adrenaline to make you stronger, faster, and more alert. Your heart pumps harder to send more blood and oxygen to your muscles, preparing you for action. At the same time, digestion slows, and your brain pauses memory and deep thinking to focus on immediate survival. While stress is great for quick reactions, staying in this state for too long can take a serious toll on your health.

Survival... to a Test?

You're probably wondering, "Why does my brain freak out about a test as if I'm being chased by a tiger?" The truth is, our brains haven't fully caught up with the modern world. They're still wired to protect us from **life-or-death threats**, even though actual tigers are no longer part of our daily lives.

Why Does Your Brain Do This?

In today's world, tests and exams have taken the place of life-threatening dangers. Society tells us that **good grades equal success**, so your brain interprets that as, "This test is *everything*! If I fail, my future is doomed!" On top of that, we've been conditioned to believe that grades reflect **how smart we are**, so doing poorly feels like a direct hit to our **self-worth**.

Even though it's just a test, your brain processes it as a **major threat** to your happiness and security. That's why your heart races, your palms sweat, and your mind blanks out. Your stress response is in full swing. Your brain is gearing up to help you survive what it thinks is a critical situation.

The Problem with This Response

Your brain is great at responding to actual danger, like dodging a speeding car, but it's not so helpful when it comes to **managing anxiety** over something like a math exam. Instead of helping, your stress response can make it harder to focus or remember what you studied, which just adds to the pressure.

What to Remember

The stress you feel before a test is your brain trying to keep you safe and secure. It's a **natural response** to what it perceives as a big threat, even though it's really just a piece of paper with questions on it. Understanding this can help you be kinder to yourself when you're feeling overwhelmed.

TL;DR

Your brain reacts to tests like they're life-or-death situations because it's wired to protect you from danger. Society makes tests feel super important for your future and self-worth, so your brain treats them as major threats. This stress response is normal, but it's also why you might feel overwhelmed or blank out—it's just your brain doing what it's designed to do.

How Do I Reduce Stress?

We all need some stress in our lives, it's a survival tool. But reducing it, especially when there's no real danger, can make things much easier to manage. Stress isn't random; it has **physiological roots**, so effective strategies work with your body's natural processes. Here are a couple of approaches that might help:

Take Deep Breaths

Yes, you've probably heard this one before: "Just breathe!" And your stressed brain might scream back, "Breathing won't make the problem go away!"

But here's why it works:

When you're stressed, your **sympathetic nervous system** (the one responsible for the "fight or flight" response) goes into overdrive, revving up your heart, tensing your muscles, and hijacking your focus. Deep belly breaths, however, stretch your **diaphragm** and can activate your **parasympathetic nervous system**—the part of your body designed to calm things down after the danger has passed.

When triggered, this system slows your heart rate and eases muscle tension, bringing you closer to a calm and balanced state. This makes it easier to think clearly, remember what you've studied, or at least feel less overwhelmed.

How to do it:

1. Sit or lie down somewhere comfortable.
2. Take a deep breath in through your nose, letting your belly expand (not your chest).
3. Exhale slowly through your mouth.
4. Repeat for a few minutes.

Humor (and Talk to Your Brain!)

Laughter is a sneaky little stress-buster. Why? Because if you're laughing, your brain gets the message that there's no real danger. After all, you wouldn't be giggling in front of a tiger, right?

Here's how to use humor:

- Watch a funny video or listen to a podcast that always cracks you up.
- Call a friend who knows how to make you laugh.
- Save memes or clips that never fail to make you smile for stressful moments.

Talk to your brain:

Sometimes, you can calm your brain down by reasoning with it, kind of like talking to an anxious friend. For example:

- "Hey, brain, it's just a piece of paper. It's not going to bite me!"
- "Chill out, silly brain. No one's dying here. Let's take this one step at a time."

Make it funny, even absurd. The more ridiculous it is, the better. For example, imagine your brain as a panicked squirrel and talk to it like you're calming it down. Adding humor makes the whole situation feel less serious, which can help reduce your stress.

Clench Your Body

When you're stressed, your body is primed to fight or flee, storing energy to deal with the perceived danger. A simple trick to release this tension is to **tense your whole body for 5-10 seconds, then let it go.** This sends a signal to your brain that the "threat" has been dealt with, helping you feel more relaxed.

Move

Physical activity works wonders for stress because it helps **release the built-up energy and tension** caused by your fight-or-flight response. Whether it's a quick walk, a short workout, or just shaking it out, moving your body can help you feel less tense and more in control.

Plan A, B, C, etc.

Sometimes, it's not the situation itself but the **fear of the unknown** that's stressful. Having multiple backup plans can ease this fear by giving you a sense of preparedness.

When things don't go as expected, knowing your next steps can reduce feelings of unpredictability and lack of control. For example, if you're waiting to hear back about a school program, plan what you'll do if you don't get accepted (apply elsewhere, try again next year, etc.). The unknown may still be stressful, but having a plan for any outcome makes it feel more manageable.

Music

Listening to music can help shift your focus away from stress and **bring your brain back to the present.** Choose music that calms or energizes you—whatever helps you reset. By focusing on the melody, rhythm, or lyrics, you give your brain a break from the stressful loop it's stuck in.

Focus on What You Can Control

One of the biggest sources of stress is **poor control**: feeling like things are happening to you, not by you. But instead of dwelling on what you *can't* control, focus on what you *can*.

For instance, if you're waiting on a test result, you can't control the grade, the teacher, or how fast they mark it. What you *can* control is how you spend your time while waiting. Take care of yourself, make backup plans, or do something that brings you joy.

Keep Experimenting

Stress management isn't one-size-fits-all. What works now might not work later, so it's helpful to have multiple tools in your kit. Keep trying until you find what works for you today, and don't be afraid to mix it up if a strategy stops being effective.

TL;DR

Stress happens, but you have tools to manage it. Tensing and relaxing your body tricks your brain into calming down. Moving your body releases built-up tension. Backup plans ease the stress of unpredictability, and music can distract your mind enough to break the stress cycle. Focus on what you can control—like your actions and mindset—rather than what's out of your hands. Small steps can make a big difference in reducing stress!

DOING YOUR BEST

Doing Your Best (or the Runner Analogy)

When people say, "Do your best," most of us hear it as, **"Do your all-time best."** But what it really means is, **"Do your best in this moment."**

Let's break it down with the **Runner Analogy.**

Imagine you're training for a 5K race. Every time you run it, your finish time varies depending on several factors: the weather, how many red lights you hit, your physical condition, or even whether you slept well the night before.

Your **all-time best** is 34 minutes and 48 seconds. But your **average time** is around 35 minutes and 10 seconds. One day, when everything went perfectly—great weather, green lights, brand-new shoes—you broke your record with 34 minutes and 27 seconds.

Now, is 34:27 your new standard? Of course not. It's just your **personal best.** Your goal isn't to beat that time every single run; it's to gradually improve your **average.**

What Does This Mean for Life?

Doing your best means doing the **best you can in the moment** with the mental, emotional, and physical resources you have at that time. It doesn't mean beating your all-time record every day.

Some days, you'll exceed your average, like when you're well-rested, stress-free, and motivated. Other days, when you're tired, distracted, or stressed, your best might fall short of your usual performance. And that's okay.

Improvement is about raising your average, not always breaking records.

What Impacts Your Best?

Life is full of factors you can't control that impact your performance:

- **Sleep:** A poor night's sleep can affect your focus and energy.
- **Stress:** When you're stressed, your brain goes into survival mode, making it harder to think clearly or remember things.
- **Physical Health:** Feeling unwell or fatigued can slow you down.

These aren't reflections of your intelligence or ability, they're just life happening.

Celebrate Progress, Not Perfection

Just because you performed better yesterday doesn't mean you have to hit that level every day. Use those peak moments as **motivation, not pressure.** If you did it once, you know it's possible. But it doesn't mean it's mandatory to reach that level every single time.

Improving yourself isn't about **being perfect every day.** It's about slowly raising your baseline over time.

So, the next time you feel like you're falling short, remind yourself: **I'm doing the best I can right now with what I have.**

TL;DR

"Doing your best" means doing the best you can in the moment, not breaking your all-time record every time. Think of it like running a 5K—some days you'll beat your personal best, and some days you won't, but the goal is to slowly improve your average.

If life throws challenges your way—poor sleep, stress, or bad luck—it's okay if your best isn't as good as yesterday. Improvement is about progress, not perfection. Remember, you're doing great! Keep going.

IMPACTS OF ADHD AND AUTISM
ON STUDIES AND LEARNING

Impacts of ADHD and autism on studies and learning

What does it actually look like to be a neurodivergent student? Let's explore how ADHD and autism can affect time in class, studying, learning, and evaluations. Don't worry, later in the book, we'll dig into workarounds to help make school life *easier* (not necessarily *easy,* but easier at least).

ADHD

Attention & Curiosity

Imagine being in a crowded room, surrounded by flashing lights, loud music, and chatter, while trying to listen to someone explaining something complicated. That's kind of what it feels like inside an ADHD brain during class.

Your mind is constantly juggling thoughts, memories, music, or your inner monologue. You're listening to the teacher, and suddenly, a random but fascinating thought pops into your head. Without realizing it, you spend a few seconds (or minutes!) following that thought while completely zoning out of the lesson. By the time you snap back, you've missed part of what was said. Now you're scrambling to catch up, but while you're trying to piece it together, you're still not paying attention. It's a cycle.

Then there's **curiosity**, which can be both a blessing and a curse. On one hand, ADHD brains are fantastic at diving deep into topics they find exciting or stimulating. But in a classroom, that same curiosity can be a distraction. A random sound or movement pulls your focus away because your brain is wired to ask, **"What's that? Is it more interesting than this?"**

On the flip side, some ADHDers find they work better by juggling multiple tasks at once. If one topic loses their attention, switching to another for a while can reignite their focus. Unfortunately, this isn't something most classroom settings allow for.

Organization & Planning

Let's be honest: the advice to **"just use a planner"** doesn't work if you don't even remember that your planner *exists.*

School revolves around structure like organizing your work, planning assignments, and prioritizing deadlines. But the ADHD brain thrives on spontaneity, not structure. This can make keeping track of homework and assignments a real struggle. And when it's time to tackle a big project, the sheer number of steps involved can feel so overwhelming that it leads to **paralysis.**

Imagine trying to write a paper. You know you need to:

1. Research.
2. Outline.
3. Write a draft.
4. Revise.
5. Format everything perfectly.

Instead of tackling these one by one, the ADHD brain sees all these steps at once, each screaming for attention. It's overwhelming, and the result is often procrastination, not because you don't care, but because you don't know where to start.

Time Perception

ADHDers often live in two time zones: **"Now"** and **"Not Now."**

This warped sense of time means you might feel like you have **all the time in the world** to finish a project... until suddenly you don't.

For example, you might start an assignment two weeks in advance but only complete about 50% of it until the last night. The distorted perception of time tricks you into thinking there's always plenty of it left, leading to rushed work, added stress, and results that reflect the crunch.

Memory

Here's the thing about memory: **we don't get to control what we forget**. It's like your brain has its own little janitor, randomly throwing stuff in the trash without asking first. You can't just decide, "I'm going to forget this embarrassing moment forever," or, "I'll never forget this math formula." (Trust me, I've tried... for both.)

It's not about struggling to remember; it's about your brain deciding what's worth keeping. And sometimes, it gets it completely wrong, like deleting the name of a book you loved while keeping that awkward comment you made in 8th grade.

Now think about how much **school leans on memory**—spelling tests, history dates, formulas. For a neurodivergent brain, especially one with ADHD, that's a lot to handle. It's not that you're not trying; your brain is just doing its own thing.

Not Stimulating Enough

Let's be real: **school isn't always a thrill ride**. For ADHDers, the need for stimulation is like a constant hunger, whether it's mental, physical, or both. Sitting through hours of lectures or worksheets? That's the fast track to boredom city.

And here's the problem: **when your brain isn't stimulated, it starts wandering.** You might not even realize it's happening until the teacher calls on you, and suddenly, you're trying to figure out if they asked about photosynthesis or last night's homework. It's not laziness; it's just that the ADHD brain thrives on interest and excitement, and sometimes school... doesn't deliver.

Why Does This Matter?

These challenges can make school life feel like swimming against the current, especially in a system designed for neurotypical brains. But recognizing these hurdles is the first step to finding solutions. ADHDers don't lack intelligence, creativity, or effort—they just need systems that work *with* their brains, not against them.

And don't worry, there's hope. In the next sections, we'll explore strategies and tips to navigate these challenges.

TL;DR:

Being a neurodivergent student with ADHD can feel like juggling flaming swords while riding a unicycle. Challenges like staying focused, managing time, and dealing with memory hiccups are part of the daily struggle.

- **Memory isn't about effort**—your brain decides what to forget, not you.
- **Boredom is the enemy**—without enough stimulation, focus evaporates.

- School isn't built for the ADHD brain, but that doesn't mean you can't find ways to thrive.

Whether it's using tools to stay organized (and remembering to check them!) or finding ways to make learning more exciting, the key is working *with* your brain—not against it.

AUTISM

The Need for Clear Instructions

For autistic students, **clear instructions are like a map**. They provide direction and security. When expectations are spelled out, they can focus on showcasing their abilities instead of second-guessing what's required.

Sure, they can deduce some information, but here's the catch: **they can't read minds.** If a teacher gives vague instructions, it leaves room for confusion. Some autistic students might ask lots of questions to clarify things (which can frustrate others), while others might stay silent out of fear or shyness, only to panic at home. Either way, it's stressful.

Communication

Communication can feel like navigating a maze. Many autistic students interpret things literally, which means **what you meant to say and what they understand might not match up**. A teacher might use a casual phrase like, "Write your thoughts on this," meaning a structured essay, but the student might think they should write exactly what's on their mind, no filter.

While subtle cues or hints work for most students, they don't always land the same way here. **It's not a lack of intelligence; it's just a different way of processing language.**

Sensory Sensitivities

Imagine trying to solve a math problem while a neon light hums like a swarm of bees, or a scratchy tag on your shirt feels like sandpaper against your skin. For autistic students, these sensory distractions can be **all-consuming**, leaving no bandwidth for learning.

It's not about being picky or dramatic. These overwhelming sensations can completely hijack their focus and energy, turning even simple tasks into a struggle.

The Power of Routine and Structure

Routine is a lifeline for autistic students. **It provides a sense of stability and control** in a world that often feels unpredictable. When routines are disrupted—like a surprise pop quiz or a new seating chart—it can cause anxiety and make it harder to concentrate.

It's not that change is impossible for them; it just takes more time and energy to adapt. Unfortunately, school doesn't always allow the space for that adjustment, which can leave them feeling unsettled and overwhelmed.

TL;DR:
- **Clear instructions** are essential—they need to know exactly what's expected to avoid unnecessary stress.
- **Communication challenges** arise when literal interpretations clash with implied meanings, so be precise.
- **Sensory sensitivities** (buzzing lights, itchy tags, loud noises) can make it hard to focus—it's not just a preference, it's a real struggle.
- **Routine and structure** help them thrive; unexpected changes can cause anxiety and throw off their focus.

The key to success? Clarity, consistency, and a bit of understanding.

HOW EDUCATORS CAN SUPPORT NEURODIVERSITY IN SCHOOL

Supporting ADHD and autistic students early on is crucial for both **inclusivity** and **normalizing neurodivergence**. When teachers and schools foster understanding, they lay the groundwork for a future where differences are embraced, not just tolerated.

This section is for teachers, educators, and school workers looking to make their classrooms more inclusive.

TALK ABOUT
NEURODIVERGENCE

Talk About Neurodivergence and Human Differences
Start by addressing the diversity of human experiences. **Explain to students that everyone is different,** not just in learning styles, but also in how they face challenges. Here's how you can approach it:

- Highlight examples they can relate to:
  "Some people have ADHD, which makes it harder to focus, but it also means they're really creative and full of energy. Others might find it hard to sit still because of their personality, or they might have tough things happening at home. But together, we can support each other."
- **Promote teamwork:** Encourage students who are doing well to help those who are struggling.

  - Assign them as "peer mentors" for activities.
  - Frame it as a win-win: **"By explaining things in different ways, you're helping others and reinforcing your own learning!"**

Everybody wins: struggling students get support, and helpers strengthen their understanding and empathy.

Normalize Neurodiversity from Day One

Start the school year with a conversation about **neurodiversity**. Make it broad and inclusive so no one feels singled out.

Here's an example script:

"Everyone has strengths and challenges, and that's what makes our classroom awesome! Some people are really great at focusing, while others have big ideas and lots of energy. Some might need quiet to work, and others love talking things through. Let's work together to help everyone shine."

Use tools like role-playing or storytelling to illustrate what it's like to experience the world differently. For example:

- Role-play scenarios where one student tries to focus in a noisy room, helping classmates empathize with sensory sensitivities.
- Create a story about a character with ADHD or autism navigating their day and discuss how their classmates support them.

Avoid Negative Labels

While ADHD and autism are disabilities, using that word with children too early can sometimes reinforce stigma. Instead, **focus on strengths and collaboration**:

- **Say this:** "Everyone's different, and that's amazing! Let's work together to make sure everyone feels supported."
- **Not this:** "Some kids have disabilities and need help from others."

By framing differences as natural, you encourage students to value diversity and help one another without judgment.

CREATING A SAFE SPACE

Let's be real: many schools proudly claim zero tolerance for bullying, but in practice, **bullying persists.** Neurodivergent kids, diagnosed or not, are often the prime targets—from subtle exclusion to outright harassment. This happens not just in elementary school but all the way through college.

A **truly safe environment** isn't about having policies that look good on paper; it's about making those policies real. That means addressing bullying head-on, training staff properly, and fostering a culture where **inclusion and respect are the norm** every day, not just during "awareness" events.

Concrete Steps for Schools

1. **Set Clear Expectations in the Classroom**:

   - Make it clear from day one that respect and kindness are non-negotiable.
   - Outline **specific consequences for bullying** so everyone knows where the line is and what happens if it's crossed.

2. **Pay Attention to Interactions**:

   - Keep an eye on how students treat each other.

○ **Proactively address subtle signs of bullying**, like exclusion, snide comments, or teasing, before they escalate.

3.   **Focus on the Bully's Perspective**:

○ Instead of just supporting the victim, work to **change the behavior of the student bullying.**
○ Help them understand how their actions impact others and provide tools to build empathy.

Be Their Safe Person

For neurodivergent kids, trust is hard to come by. **They learn early that people might not be on their side,** even when they report bullying. That's where you come in.

Your role as a teacher goes beyond instruction:

- **Be the adult they can trust** to protect them.
- Create an environment where they know their concerns will be taken seriously and their well-being is a top priority.

When students feel safe coming to you, they're more likely to report problems before they spiral. This doesn't just help the individual—it improves the overall classroom dynamic.

Every student deserves a safe and smooth school experience. However, **neurodivergent students face additional challenges** that make them more vulnerable to bullying, misunderstandings, and trauma. This isn't about saying they're more important, it's about recognizing that their risk is higher, and **schools need to prioritize their safety and well-being.**

When neurodivergent students experience bullying or feel unsupported, the long-term effects can go beyond school, leading to **self-esteem struggles, anxiety, or difficulty advocating for themselves as adults.**

The Problem With Punishing Victims Who Defend Themselves

Here's a harsh truth: schools often punish victims of bullying who finally stand up for themselves, while the bully gets little more than a warning. This sends the wrong message: **"Defending yourself only makes things worse."**

What does this teach kids? That their voice doesn't matter. That fighting back, even after months or years of harassment, makes them the problem. Over time, this mindset can create adults who **struggle to set boundaries or advocate for themselves.**

When a bullied student retaliates, it's not aggression, it's **survival mode.** They've endured so much that they feel they have no other option. Instead of punishing them, schools should:

- **Recognize the context** of their actions.
- Provide support to help them heal from the trauma of ongoing bullying.

Supporting Both Victims and Bullies

Bullying is never okay, but **the bully needs help too.** Often, their actions stem from deeper issues, such as challenges at home, insecurity, or struggles with emotional regulation. Addressing these root causes can lead to real change.

Here's how schools can support both sides:

- **For the victim:**

○ Build a network of loving, supportive adults who listen and advocate for them.
○ Teach effective coping strategies to rebuild their confidence and sense of safety.

- **For the bully:**

  ○ Use guidance and interventions to address the underlying causes of their behavior.
  ○ Teach healthier ways to express their emotions or cope with challenges.

Collaboration with parents or guardians is also key. By working together, schools and families can reinforce positive behavior changes. However, it's important to acknowledge that sometimes **the bullying starts at home**, and additional support systems may be needed.

People naturally respond better to encouragement than punishment. **Punishment might stop bad behavior temporarily**, but it rarely teaches what to do instead. On the other hand, **positive reinforcement highlights what's working and encourages more of it.**

In the classroom, this means:

- **Celebrating acts of kindness and support**: When students help one another or show respect, acknowledge it publicly.
- **Rewarding positive behavior**: This doesn't have to be a big prize, even a heartfelt "I saw how you helped today, and it was awesome" can make a difference.

By focusing on what students are doing right, you're **creating a ripple effect** of good behavior. Kindness becomes the norm, and students are less likely to bully when they see that helping others is valued.

When Bullying Gets Serious

Sometimes, bullying persists despite a positive classroom culture. **This is when counselors or psychologists should step in.** They can:

- Work one-on-one with victims to help them process their experiences and regain confidence.
- Address the deeper issues behind a bully's behavior, offering tools to manage emotions and relationships more effectively.

TL;DR:
1. **Zero tolerance isn't enough**: Bullying persists without active intervention and a culture of inclusion.
2. **Reinforce good behavior**: Celebrate kindness and reward positive actions to encourage a supportive environment.
3. **Support both victims and bullies**: Address the root causes of bullying while helping victims heal and thrive.
4. **Involve professionals if needed**: School counselors or psychologists can offer deeper support to both sides.

True safety isn't about punishment—it's about teaching kindness, empathy, and respect. By focusing on the positive and addressing issues compassionately, schools can create spaces where every student feels valued and secure.

The Power of a Safe Space

Having a designated safe space in school is a **game-changer for neurodivergent students.** It's not just a room; it's a place where they can breathe, reset, and feel understood. When things get overwhelming, whether it's sensory overload, social stress, or frustration, this "chill zone" can be the difference between powering through the day or completely shutting down.

Why it works:

- It gives students a sense of control over their environment.
- It validates their needs and shows that the school cares about their well-being.
- It helps them regulate emotions and return to class ready to learn.

What Should the Space Include?

You don't need anything fancy, just a cozy, calming area with a few tools to help students feel safe. Here's a simple list:

- **Noise-canceling headphones:** Block out overwhelming sounds.
- **Music or white noise options:** Provide soothing alternatives to loud environments.
- **Coloring** books **or drawing supplies:** Engage the hands and calm the mind.
- **Fidget toys:** Help with focus and sensory regulation.
- **Soft lighting and comfy seating:** Create a relaxing atmosphere.

Bonus: Keep the space inviting but not overstimulating. Neutral tones, soft textures, and minimal clutter go a long way.

How to Use the Safe Space

- **Set clear guidelines**: Let students know they can use the room when they feel overwhelmed, but also explain how to communicate this need (e.g., raising a specific card or signaling the teacher).
- **Keep it accessible**: Don't make students feel like they need a "big reason" to use the space—sometimes they just need a break, and that's okay.
- **Check in afterward**: A quick, nonjudgmental conversation can help students feel supported and ready to rejoin the class.

23

IN THE CLASSROOM

Creating a Neurodivergent-Friendly Classroom

Kids and teenagers spend most of their day in the classroom, so **it's essential to make it a safe, inclusive, and supportive environment** for everyone—neurodivergent or not. Even if there's only one neurodivergent student, setting up accommodations benefits the entire class.

Here's why:

- **It supports neurodivergent students** and makes them feel seen, valued, and understood.
- **It teaches neurotypical students to be more inclusive**, fostering understanding they'll carry into their adult lives and workplaces.

When kids grow up in environments where inclusivity is the norm, they're more likely to **create positive, accessible spaces in the future**, and that's how we change the world step by step.

Movement Breaks: A Small Change, Big Results

Sitting still for hours? It's hard for *anyone*, but it's especially challenging for neurodivergent students like those with ADHD. Their bodies and brains need movement to stay engaged and focused.

Sure, there's recess, but let's be honest, **recess is the bare minimum**. A small but impactful improvement would be to introduce **5-minute movement breaks** throughout the day.

Why it works:

- It helps kids reset and release energy.
- Focus and productivity improve for *everyone*.
- It makes school more enjoyable and aligned with kids' natural needs.

Ideas for movement breaks:

- Quick stretches or jumping jacks.
- A short walk around the classroom.
- Fun challenges like "touch 5 objects that are blue."

Flexible Seating: Making Comfort Inclusive

Traditional seating isn't designed for neurodivergent brains and bodies. For kids with ADHD, **sitting "properly" takes energy and focus**, which leaves them with less attention for actual learning. Imagine trying to focus on a math lesson while also fighting the urge to squirm or fidget... it's exhausting.

Flexible seating options help kids feel more comfortable and **reduce the energy spent "just sitting still."** It also sends a clear message: their needs are valid, and they're supported.

Easy options to try:

- Wiggle cushions or balance balls.
- Standing desks or wobble stools.
- Floor seating with cushions.
- Allowing students to work in different areas of the classroom when appropriate.

When you provide these options, you're not just accommodating one student, you're improving the learning experience for everyone. **Comfort boosts focus, safety, and trust in the classroom.**

Supporting Neurodivergent Students: Clear Instructions, Flexibility, and Inclusive Assessments

1. Provide Clear, Structured Instructions

Clear and structured instructions **benefit everyone**, not just neurodivergent students. When tasks are broken into **step-by-step instructions**, students know exactly what's expected, which reduces stress and confusion.

- **Written step-by-step guidance** ensures tasks are easy to follow.
- **Teach task division**: Show the class how to break a large assignment into smaller, manageable steps. This is a skill that will help them for life.

2. Use Visual Aids to Keep Students on Track

Visual tools like schedules, charts, and diagrams are powerful learning aids for all students, especially those with ADHD and autism.

- **Why visuals work**: They simplify information, keep students organized, and offer a consistent reference point.
- Examples: Visual schedules for the day, diagrams to explain processes, or checklists to mark completed steps.

3. Positive Reinforcement Over Punishment

Humans learn better with praise and positive reinforcement than with punishment. Recognizing students' efforts, even the small ones, builds confidence, motivation, and connection to the class.

- **Praise specific actions**: "Great job on breaking the project into steps!"
- **Highlight helpful behavior**: Celebrate students supporting their classmates or completing tasks independently.

For ADHD students especially, being recognized for their efforts validates their contributions and motivates them to keep trying.

4. Mix Up Activities to Keep Engagement High

ADHD brains thrive on **intellectual stimulation**. Sitting through repetitive tasks can cause boredom, which makes focus nearly impossible.

- Alternate between activities: A short discussion, followed by hands-on learning, then an interactive quiz.
- Use creative exercises: Incorporate drawing, storytelling, or building something related to the lesson.

Keeping activities fresh helps ADHD students stay engaged while also making learning more fun for the whole class.

5. Be Flexible With Assessments

Traditional, timed tests are a nightmare for many ADHD students. The pressure to perform quickly can increase stress, reduce focus, and negatively impact memory, leading to lower grades that don't reflect what they truly know.

Here's what teachers can do:

- **Offer extra time**: It reduces stress and allows students to complete the test without rushing.

- **Break tests into smaller sections**: Include short breaks in between. This helps maintain focus and manage time better.
- **Use alternative assessments**: Let students demonstrate their knowledge through:
  - Projects
  - Oral presentations
  - One-on-one discussions
  - Creative assignments (e.g., artwork, videos, or story-based explanations).

Why does this matter? Assessments should measure knowledge, not speed under pressure. Breaking the test into manageable parts or offering different formats makes evaluation fairer and more inclusive.

6. Address the Root of Cheating

The reality is that **students cheat because, in our society, grades take priority over learning**. If a student struggles and sees no alternative, they might resort to cheating just to "fit in" and avoid being seen as different.

Solutions to reduce cheating:

- Focus on learning over grades. Celebrate understanding and progress, not just scores.
- Offer multiple ways to validate knowledge: projects, creative assignments, or one-on-one discussions.
- Include short movement or stretching breaks during tests to reduce stress and improve focus. Even silent breaks work to prevent sharing answers.

By addressing why students feel forced to cheat, we **shift the classroom culture** to prioritize growth, understanding, and fairness.

Creating an Inclusive Classroom: Helping ADHD Students Thrive

Kids and teens spend most of their day at school. That's why it's so important to create a **classroom environment where everyone feels safe, supported, and able to succeed.** Even if there's just **one neurodivergent student**, these changes benefit the entire class by teaching empathy, flexibility, and inclusivity.

Supporting ADHD Students Through Small Changes

1. **Understand Their Behaviors as Part of Learning**

    - ADHD behaviors (like fidgeting, movement, or needing frequent breaks) aren't disruptions; they're strategies the student uses to focus.
    - **Reframing this mindset** helps teachers see these actions as tools, not problems.

2. **Encourage Open Communication**

    - Let students know they can safely express their needs without judgment.
    - Build trust by being their "safe person": someone they know will listen, understand, and advocate for them.

3. **Highlight Strengths, Not Just Challenges**

    - ADHD students often feel they're "not good enough" or "annoying" just for existing. Break that cycle by **celebrating their strengths**:

- Creative thinking
- Problem-solving in hands-on activities
- Energetic ideas and unique approaches to tasks

○ Recognizing their successes **boosts self-esteem** and helps them see their ADHD as part of their strengths, not just struggles.

4. **Create a Supportive Environment**

○ **Normalize mistakes**: Shift the focus from failure to learning opportunities.
  - When students know they won't be judged harshly, they feel safer taking risks and engaging in class.
○ Positive reinforcement (like praising effort, celebrating kindness, and recognizing small wins) builds confidence and motivation.

5. **Make Learning Accessible**

○ Simple adjustments like:
  - **Movement breaks**: Short, frequent breaks keep energy in check and improve focus.
  - **Flexible seating**: Options like wobble stools or cushions make it easier for ADHD students to stay comfortable and attentive.
  - **Clear, structured instructions**: Step-by-step, written guidance reduces stress and helps everyone stay on task.
○ **Rethink assessments**: Time limits can be stressful and unfair. Offering extra time or alternative formats (projects, oral presentations, creative assignments) allows ADHD students to **demonstrate their understanding** without added pressure.

The Bigger Picture: Building Empathy and Inclusivity

Inclusive classrooms benefit everyone, not just neurodivergent students. When teachers actively support ADHD students, the rest of the class learns to:

- Be more understanding of differences.
- Celebrate strengths in themselves and others.
- Carry empathy and respect into their adult lives.

This creates a **ripple effect**: classrooms that embrace diversity help build a society where differences are seen as strengths, not flaws.

TL;DR:

1. **Reframe ADHD behaviors** as part of the learning process, not disruptions.
2. **Celebrate strengths** to boost confidence and break the "not good enough" mindset.
3. Create a **safe, supportive environment** where mistakes are learning opportunities and communication is encouraged.
4. Make learning accessible with **movement breaks**, flexible seating, clear instructions, and alternative assessments.
5. Foster a culture of **empathy and inclusivity**, preparing students to value differences in school and beyond.

With understanding, patience, and small changes, teachers can help ADHD students—and all students—thrive in a supportive, inclusive classroom.

24

SOME TIPS FOR AUTISTIC STUDENTS

Supporting Autistic Students: Communication, Understanding, and Stability

All the tips and tricks we shared for ADHD students can also be used for autistic students.

Here are a short list of behaviors to adopt specifically with autistic students.

Clear, Literal Communication

Autistic students process language **literally**, so avoid ambiguous phrases or unclear instructions. For example:

- **Instead of saying**: "Get started whenever you're ready."
- **Say**: "Start working on page 5 now."

If a student seems confused, **avoid dismissive responses** like, *"I just explained it; you need to listen."* Autistic students *are* listening, but they may need the explanation framed differently. Instead:

- Ask: "What part feels unclear?"

- Rephrase using simpler terms, step-by-step instructions, or analogies. Autistic students often find analogies helpful!

Be Patient With Communication

- Allow **extra time** for students to process information and respond.
- Be open to alternative communication, like written responses or gestures, if verbal communication feels too difficult.

Important: If an autistic student freezes up, don't insist they talk, it can escalate their stress. Offer a calm, nonjudgmental space and give them time.

Understanding Shutdowns and Meltdowns

Both are **defense mechanisms** when an autistic brain is overloaded. These are not choices; they are involuntary responses to extreme emotional stress.

1. **Shutdowns**

     ◦ The brain "shuts down" to cope. Students might:
          ▪ Appear paralyzed, unable to move, speak, or respond.
          ▪ Communicate only by text or gestures (if able).
     ◦ What to do:
          ▪ Stay calm and patient.
          ▪ Remove any additional stressors (loud sounds, bright lights).
          ▪ Allow time and space for recovery.

2. **Meltdowns**

- The brain triggers a "fight" response due to distress. Students might scream, throw things, hit themselves or others.
- **What helps varies**: Some may need firm physical reassurance (like a tight hug), while for others, **touch can make it worse.**
- **Ask parents (or the student, if they are old enough to understand their meltdowns) in advance** about the best strategies for handling meltdowns for that specific student.

Minimizing Unexpected Changes

Surprise = **stress** for autistic students, even if they're fully prepared for the activity.

- **Give advance notice** for any schedule or routine changes. For example:
    - "Tomorrow, we're having a test. Here's what to expect."
    - "Next week, we're going on a field trip to the museum."
- Clearly explain the change and what it means for the student.

By reducing surprises, you help autistic students feel more secure and better prepared to handle transitions.

TL;DR:
1. **Use clear, literal language** and avoid ambiguous phrases. If they're confused, rephrase with patience, don't dismiss their concerns.
2. **Be patient with communication**: Allow extra time to process and respond; accept alternative forms of communication.
3. **Understand shutdowns and meltdowns**: These are involuntary. Speak to parents to learn how to support the student best.
    - **Shutdowns**: The student may freeze and become unresponsive.

- ◦ **Meltdowns**: The student may scream or hit out of distress.
4. **Minimize unexpected changes**: Give advance notice for schedule changes or tests, and explain them clearly.

These strategies—paired with compassion and understanding—create a classroom where autistic students feel safe, supported, and able to thrive.

25

HUMAN RESOURCES TO HELP

How College Academic Advisors Can Support Neurodivergent Students

More Than Just Picking Classes

Let's be honest: college is tough, and for neurodivergent students, the challenges can go far beyond the classroom. Academic advisors who truly **understand neurodivergence** can make a world of difference by offering support that's both practical and personalized.

Here's how they can help:

1. **Building the Right Schedule**
   - Advisors can help you create a course schedule that avoids overload and unnecessary stress.
   - They ensure you take the classes you need (and skip the ones you don't), which keeps you on track to graduate without burnout.
   - **Why this matters**: College structure can feel chaotic. A well-organized schedule gives you **clarity** and a sense of control.

Life Skills That Make College Easier

College isn't just about academics, it's also about building routines and managing responsibilities. Advisors can:

- Help you create a **weekly routine** to stay organized. This is huge if you thrive on structure to manage deadlines and priorities.
- Offer regular check-ins to act as a **low-key accountability partner**. These meetings can keep you on track, help you tackle small problems early, and celebrate your wins.

Think of them as someone in your corner, motivating you when things get tough and helping you navigate the challenges before they snowball.

Connecting You to Campus Life

The social side of college can feel overwhelming, especially if you're neurodivergent. Advisors can help by:

- Suggesting **extracurricular activities** that align with your strengths and interests: clubs, sports, volunteer opportunities, or student groups.
- Giving you that **gentle push** to take the first step to join. Whether it's finding a club that feels right or introducing you to someone, advisors can help bridge the gap.

Why it matters: Feeling connected to campus life makes a huge difference. It's not just about meeting people, it's about building a sense of community, which can make college feel less isolating.

How Counselors Support Neurodivergent Students

Adjusting to High School or College

Starting high school or college can feel like being dropped into a whole new world: new routines, new expectations, and sometimes, living away from home for the first time. For neurodivergent students, this adjustment can be even more overwhelming. **Counseling centers** are like a safe haven during this time.

Here's why they're so important:

- **They provide judgment-free support**: Whether it's stress, homesickness, workload anxiety, or struggling to balance it all, counselors are there to listen and help you process what's going on.
- **They help you navigate big changes**: The first few weeks in a new environment are often the toughest. Counselors can guide you through this adjustment, offering tools to manage your emotions and stress levels.

Practical Help When You Need It

Counseling centers don't just offer a listening ear. They also provide practical tools to help you thrive. Some ways they can support you include:

- **Time Management**: Helping you plan and structure your day so you don't feel overwhelmed.
- **Conflict Resolution**: Guiding you through roommate issues, friendship struggles, or miscommunications.

- **Stress Management**: Offering techniques to handle anxiety, workload stress, or sensory overload (which can be especially challenging for autistic or ADHD students).

Why this matters: Neurodivergent students often face unique challenges, like balancing overstimulation with new demands, so having **tailored strategies** can make all the difference.

A Resource Hub

If you're feeling lost or unsure where to go for help, **counselors can connect you to the right campus resources.** Whether it's academic support, accessibility services, or social groups, they'll help you find what you need.

This way, you don't have to navigate the overwhelming options on your own.

Thriving, Not Just Surviving

The ultimate goal of counseling centers is to help you **not just survive school, but actually enjoy it and thrive**. By offering:

- Emotional support,
- Practical life tools, and
- A safe, judgment-free space to talk,

counselors become a **solid support system** as you settle into this new chapter. They help you take things one step at a time, so you can feel more confident, secure, and capable.

How Tutors Can Help Neurodivergent Students Thrive

Personalized Learning That Makes Sense

Struggling with a subject or feeling lost in class? **Tutors can be a game-changer.** They're like your personal guide, breaking things down at **your pace** in ways that actually make sense to *you*. Instead of trying to keep up with the rest of the class, tutors focus on:

- The areas where you need the most help.
- Using strategies and explanations tailored to **how your brain works**.

This means you're not just playing catch-up, you're building a stronger understanding of the subject and **getting ahead**.

Building Better Study Habits

Sometimes, school struggles aren't about understanding the content, it's about how you approach learning. A good tutor can:

- Teach you how to **organize notes and materials** in a way that works for you.
- Help with **time management** so you can stay on top of deadlines and study efficiently.
- Share strategies for tackling **tricky subjects or test anxiety** (like breaking tasks into smaller steps or using memory aids).

These skills don't just help in one class; they set you up for success throughout school and beyond.

Boosting Your Confidence

One of the best parts about working with a tutor is the confidence boost you get when things *finally click*.

- Concepts that once felt impossible start to make sense.
- You feel **capable** of taking on challenges instead of avoiding them.

This confidence doesn't stop at the classroom door, it spills into other parts of your life, too, helping you approach challenges with a new mindset.

Finding the Right Tutor for You

For neurodivergent students, it's especially helpful to find a tutor who **shares your neurotype** or understands how your brain works. Why?

- They can relate to your struggles and offer strategies that **worked for them**.
- They're more likely to explain things in a way that clicks with your thought process.

When a tutor understands you, the learning process becomes smoother and much more enjoyable.

TL;DR:
- **Academic Advisors**: More than class schedulers, they help balance your workload, create routines, and connect you with clubs or activities that match your interests. They're your personal guide for school *and* life.

- **Counselors**: High school or college can feel overwhelming, but counselors are there to support you through stress, homesickness, and big life changes. They make sure you don't just survive, but thrive.
- **Tutors**: Stuck on a tricky subject? Tutors break down material in a way that makes sense, teach you study habits, and boost your confidence. They're your personal guide to staying on track and succeeding in school.

Finding support from advisors, counselors, and tutors can make school less stressful and help you feel more confident, organized, and capable.

LEARNING AND STUDIES

We are now jumping into the core of the subject for this book. Learning and studying as an ADHD student. In this section, we will talk about active learning, motivation, procrastination, tips, tricks, and workarounds to help you study, as well as some cognitive biases that can be obstacles to your learning.

26

BASIC NEEDS

I t's important to remember: even though young people are like sponges when it comes to learning, **learning is *not* a basic human need.** To be ready to absorb information, your **basic needs** have to be met first.

So, what are these needs? Let's break it down.

1. Food and Water

Your brain is like a **high-performance engine**, and food and water are its fuel.

- Without enough **healthy food**, it's harder to:
  - Focus on lessons.
  - Remember what you've learned.
  - Stay awake and alert during the day.
- **Dehydration** makes it worse. When you're low on water, your brain struggles to function, and concentrating feels like climbing a mountain.

2. Shelter

Having a **safe and stable place to live** is a fundamental need.

- If you're worried about where you'll sleep tonight or whether you're safe, your brain shifts into **survival mode**.
- Survival mode takes up all your mental energy, leaving **no space** to focus on school, homework, or tests.

3. Sleep

Sleep is like **recharging your brain's battery**. Without enough of it, everything gets harder:

- Your memory becomes fuzzy.
- Focusing feels impossible.
- Stress becomes overwhelming.

But when you get **a full night's sleep**, your brain:

- Processes and remembers information better.
- Stays alert and ready to learn.
- Handles challenges and stress more effectively.

4. Clothing

Wearing clothes that are right for the weather is more important than you might think.

- Imagine trying to take a test while you're:
    - **Freezing** in a cold classroom.
    - **Sweating** through your shirt on a hot day.
- Being too hot, cold, or uncomfortable takes your focus away from learning.

The Brain's First Question

B efore your brain is ready to learn, it always asks:
"Are my basic needs met?"

If the answer is "no", because you're hungry, tired, unsafe, or un-comfortable, your brain will focus on **survival**, not schoolwork.

TL;DR: Basic Needs Before Learning

To be ready to learn, your **basic needs** must be met first:

1. **Food and water**: Fuel for focus, memory, and energy.
2. **Shelter**: A safe, stable home reduces stress and frees up mental energy for learning.
3. **Sleep**: Rest recharges your brain, improving focus, memory, and stress management.
4. **Clothing**: Being dressed for the weather keeps you comfortable and focused.

When these needs are met, your brain can **shift its focus from survival to thriving**, opening the door for learning and growth.

Safety and Security Needs: The Next Step for Learning

Once your **basic physiological needs** (food, water, sleep, shelter) are met, your brain asks:

"Am I safe?"

If the answer is *no*, your mind shifts its focus to survival mode, making it nearly impossible to concentrate on learning. Feeling safe, physically, emotionally, and financially, creates the stability you need to focus, grow, and thrive in school.

1. Personal Safety

When you feel safe at home, in your community, and at school, it's much easier to:

- Focus on your studies.
- Relax, think clearly, and ask for help when you need it.
- Stay motivated to engage in class or complete assignments.

But if safety feels uncertain, your brain can't prioritize learning. Constant stress or worry about your environment eats up mental energy, leaving little room for focusing on school.

2. Physical Health

Your health and learning are deeply connected. When you're physically healthy:

- You have the **energy** to pay attention in class, do homework, and participate in activities.
- Your brain works better, so you can **focus, retain information, and solve problems** more easily.

But if you're dealing with sickness, exhaustion, or chronic health issues, everything gets harder:

- Concentrating feels impossible.
- Memory and motivation dip.
- Tasks that were once easy can feel overwhelming.

3. Financial Stability

Money stress doesn't just affect your future, it impacts your ability to focus **right now**.

- Worrying about finances can be a huge distraction, making it hard to concentrate or stay motivated.
- Financial stability allows you to access the tools you need to succeed, like:
    - Books and technology
    - Extracurricular activities
    - Quiet, supportive study spaces

With fewer financial worries, you can focus on **learning, not just surviving**.

The Brain's Second Question: "Am I Safe?"

If the answer to this question is *no*, whether because of personal safety, health, or financial instability, your brain prioritizes survival over growth.

TL;DR: Safety and Security Needs Before Learning

1. **Personal safety**: Feeling safe at home, school, and in your community gives you the peace of mind to focus and stay motivated.
2. **Physical health**: Good health fuels focus, energy, and memory, while illness makes it harder to learn and succeed.

3. **Financial stability**: Less stress about money allows you to access resources, participate in activities, and focus on your education.

Once your brain knows you're safe, it can shift from survival mode to learning mode, unlocking your potential to succeed.

Love and Belongingness: The Power of Connection in Learning

When you feel loved, supported, and connected, whether it's from family, friends, or your community, it makes a **huge difference** in how you approach learning and life.

- **Confidence Boost**: Knowing people care about you makes you believe in yourself, even when things get tough.
- **Motivation**: Your "cheering squad" keeps you going when you're tempted to give up.
- **Stress Relief**: Feeling connected reduces anxiety and makes it easier to focus on schoolwork.

A supportive environment empowers you to take risks, ask questions, and engage fully in your learning. Instead of worrying about whether you belong, you can focus on growing and succeeding.

The Brain's Third Question: "Am I Loved?"

If the answers to the first two questions ("Are my basic needs met?" and "Am I safe?") are *yes*, your brain will then ask:

"Am I loved? Do I belong?"

When you can answer *yes*, you feel secure, connected, and ready to focus on your studies. But if the answer is *no*, learning becomes a challenge because feelings of loneliness or rejection take up emotional space.

When Needs Aren't Fully Met

It's okay to admit that **life isn't always easy**, especially when your basic needs, safety, or sense of belonging aren't fully met.

- If your family struggles financially or emotionally, there may be limits to what you can change. **That's not your fault.**
- When school feels extra hard, remember this: **It's normal to struggle when your needs aren't met.** You're not failing, you're doing your best in a difficult situation.

Focus on What You Can Control

Even small steps can help you feel a bit more supported and connected:

- **Lean on people who care**: friends, teachers, counselors, or mentors who make you feel seen and heard.
- **Be kind to yourself**: It's okay if you're not performing perfectly when things are tough.
- **Celebrate small wins**: Even showing up and trying your best counts as progress.

TL;DR:

1. **Food and Water**: Your brain needs good fuel to focus, stay awake, and remember things. Healthy food and clean water keep you sharp.
2. **Shelter**: A safe, stable place to live gives you the peace of mind to concentrate on school.
3. **Sleep**: Rest recharges your brain, improving focus, energy, and stress management.
4. **Clothing**: Wearing weather-appropriate clothes keeps you comfortable and less distracted.
5. **Safety**: Feeling safe at home, school, and in your community lets you focus and stay motivated.
6. **Health**: Physical health gives you the energy and stamina to tackle schoolwork.
7. **Financial Stability**: Less stress about money means better access to resources and fewer distractions.

8. **Love and Support**: Feeling cared for by family or friends builds confidence, reduces stress, and keeps you motivated.

If these needs aren't fully met, it's normal to struggle with learning. Focus on what you *can* fix, and be kind to yourself, you're doing your best, and that's what really counts.

27

COGNITIVE BIASES

Your brain is a supercomputer, constantly processing an overwhelming amount of information. To handle all of this efficiently, it relies on **shortcuts**: patterns or strategies that have worked before.

Here's the catch:

- While shortcuts save time and energy, they don't always lead to the best decisions or right reasoning.
- Sometimes, your brain applies **old solutions to new problems**, even when they're not the right fit.

These mental shortcuts are called **cognitive biases**, and they can influence your thoughts, decisions, and actions, often without you even realizing it.

What Is a Bias?

A **bias** is like a mental lens that shapes how you see the world.

- It's a tendency to favor certain ideas, people, or approaches over others.
- Biases can be **conscious** (you're aware of them) or **unconscious** (hidden but still affecting you).

While not all biases are bad, some can **negatively impact your learning** by making you:

- Jump to conclusions.
- Ignore better solutions.
- Judge situations or people unfairly.

Why Should You Care About Biases?

When you understand how biases work, you can:

- **Spot them** in your own thinking.
- Challenge old habits or assumptions that hold you back.
- "Rewire" your brain to make better, more accurate decisions.

In short, **knowing your biases** can help you become a more effective learner, problem-solver, and goal-getter.

What's Next?

There are **hundreds of cognitive biases**, but don't worry, we'll focus on the ones that are most likely to impact your learning. By recognizing these biases, you can adjust your thinking and unlock smarter ways to tackle challenges.

Remember: Your brain's shortcuts are automatic, but with awareness and practice, you can take control and use them to your advantage.

Stay tuned! We'll break down key cognitive biases, show you how they work, and give you tools to overcome them so you can **learn better and achieve your goals**.

Confirmation Bias

Confirmation bias happens when you only focus on information that supports what you already believe and ignore or dismiss anything that challenges it. It's like your brain saying, *"See? I was right all along!"* even when that belief might not be accurate.

How It Shows Up in Learning

Let's say you believe:

- *"I'm terrible at math."*

Here's how confirmation bias plays out:

- When you struggle with a math problem, you **notice** it and say, *"See? I knew it. I'm bad at this."*
- But when you get a problem right, you dismiss it as **luck** or think it was just "too easy."

Over time, this bias reinforces your belief and makes you feel worse about yourself, even if it's not true. The more you believe it, the less motivated you are to try.

How to Overcome Confirmation Bias

1.   **Start Noticing Your Wins**

     - Actively look for times when you succeed, no matter how small.
     - Write them down to create "proof" that challenges your negative belief. For example: *"I got 3 questions right today.*

That's not luck, that's progress!"

2.   Question Your Thoughts

- When you catch yourself thinking, *"I'm terrible at this,"* ask:
  - *"Is that really true, or am I just focusing on the negatives?"*
  - *"What's one example where I did well?"*

3.   Reframe Your Mindset

- Instead of thinking, *"I'm bad at math,"* try saying:
  - *"I'm working on improving my math skills."*
  - *"It's okay to make mistakes while I'm learning."*

4.   Celebrate Progress, Not Perfection

- Success doesn't mean getting everything right. It's about **improving over time**. Notice and celebrate small steps forward, like understanding a concept you struggled with before.

Fixed Mindset

A **fixed mindset** is when you believe that your abilities, intelligence, and talents are set in stone, like they're something you're born with and can't change.

For example, you might think:

- *"I'm just not good at science, and I never will be."*
- *"If I fail this, it proves I'm not smart."*

With a fixed mindset, challenges and mistakes feel like proof of your limits, which can make you:

- **Avoid challenges** altogether.
- Give up easily when things get tough.
- Feel stuck and lose motivation.

How a Fixed Mindset Holds You Back

1. **Fear of Failure**: If you're convinced failure means you're not capable, you'll avoid taking risks or trying new things.
2. **Avoiding Challenges**: You might stick to what you're already good at because challenges feel like threats, not opportunities.
3. **Struggling to Bounce Back**: Setbacks can feel overwhelming because they confirm the negative beliefs you already have about yourself.
4. **Stunted Growth**: By putting limits on yourself before you even try, you miss out on chances to learn and grow.

The Alternative: Growth Mindset

The good news? You can **shift to a growth mindset**, which means believing that your abilities can improve with effort, practice, and time.

Fixed mindset says: *"I can't do this."*

Growth mindset says: *"I can't do this yet, but I'm working on it."*

How to Shift Your Mindset

1. **Reframe Failure**

    ◦ See mistakes as part of the learning process, not as proof you're not capable.
    ◦ Say to yourself: *"What can I learn from this?"*

2. **Focus on Effort, Not Talent**

    ◦ Celebrate hard work and progress, not just results.
    ◦ Example: Instead of thinking, *"I'm bad at math,"* think, *"I'm improving by practicing a little every day."*

3. **Add "Yet" to Negative Thoughts**

    ◦ Replace: *"I can't do this."*
    ◦ With: *"I can't do this **yet**."* It reminds you that growth takes time.

4. **Embrace Challenges**

    ◦ Think of challenges as opportunities to grow, not threats to your abilities.

Self-Serving Bias

Self-serving bias happens when you:

- Take credit for your successes: *"I aced that test because I'm super smart!"*
- Blame outside factors for your failures: *"I failed because the test was too hard, not because I didn't study enough."*

While this bias can protect your self-esteem in the short term, it also **stops you from improving** because you don't see where you need to learn or grow. It's like wearing blinders that only let you notice the things that make you look good.

How It Holds You Back

1. **Stops Growth**

    ○ By blaming failures on external factors, you miss opportunities to figure out what went wrong and how to improve.
    ○ Example: If you blame a failed math test on bad luck instead of your study habits, you won't adjust how you prepare next time.

2. **Distorts Reality**

    ○ It feels good to think you're naturally talented when things go well, but this can stop you from working hard to develop your skills.
    ○ Reality check: Success often comes from effort, preparation, and learning, not just luck or natural ability.

3. **Limits Accountability**

- Self-serving bias lets you avoid responsibility when things go wrong. But without accountability, it's tough to grow, learn, or reach your goals.

How to Overcome Self-Serving Bias

1. **Be Honest With Yourself**

- After a success or failure, ask:
  - *"What did I do well?"*
  - *"What could I have done better?"*
- Recognize both the **effort you put in** and **areas where you can improve**.

2. **Focus on Learning, Not Blame**

- When something goes wrong, shift from blaming to learning.
  - Instead of: *"The teacher made the test too hard."*
  - Try: *"I didn't study enough, so next time, I'll review earlier."*

3. **Celebrate Effort Over Luck**

- When you succeed, focus on the work you put in, not just the result.
  - Example: *"I did well because I practiced and prepared for this."*

4. **Ask for Feedback**

° Sometimes it's hard to see our blind spots. Ask teachers, mentors, or friends for feedback so you can get a more balanced view of what you're doing well and where you can improve.

Sunk Cost Fallacy

The **sunk cost fallacy** happens when you stick with something—whether it's a study method, activity, or even a relationship—just because you've already invested time, energy, or effort into it, **even if it's not working anymore**.

For example:

- You keep using a study method that doesn't help because you've already spent hours trying to make it work.
- You stay in a club or activity you no longer enjoy because you've spent months being part of it.
- You force yourself to finish a boring movie just because you're halfway through.
- You force yourself to stay in a program that doesn't fit you anymore because you've already did a few semesters and you don't want to start over again.

In all these cases, you're holding on because of what you've already "sunk" into it, not because it's actually helping or making you happy.

Why It Holds You Back

1. **Wasted Time and Energy**

    ◦ By sticking with something that isn't working, you're losing valuable time and energy you could spend on something more effective or enjoyable.

2. **Stops You From Improving**

  ◦ Forcing yourself to keep using a bad study method won't help you learn better, it just keeps you stuck.

3.   **Guilt Over Letting Go**

  ◦ It's easy to feel like quitting equals failure, but sometimes **quitting is the smartest choice**.

How to Overcome the Sunk Cost Fallacy

1.   **Ask Yourself: "Is This Helping Me?"**

  ◦ Be honest: Is this activity, method, path or task actually benefiting you?
  ◦ If the answer is no, it's okay to let it go.

2.   **Focus on the Future, Not the Past**

  ◦ The time and energy you've already spent are **gone**, you can't get them back.
  ◦ Instead, focus on what's best for you **moving forward**.

3.   **Reframe Letting Go**

  ◦ Quitting something that isn't working isn't failure, it's **making a smart decision** to free up space for better options.
  ◦ Example: *"This study method didn't work, so I'm going to try a new approach that actually helps me learn."*

4.   **Cut Your Losses Early**

- The sooner you realize something isn't serving you, the better. Don't let the time you've already "invested" trick you into sticking with it.

Spotlight Effect

The **spotlight effect** is when you believe everyone is paying way more attention to you than they actually are. You feel like there's a giant spotlight on you, highlighting every little thing you do: mistakes, awkward moments, or what you're wearing.

But here's the truth:

- Most people are **too busy worrying about themselves** to notice what you're doing.
- What feels huge to you (like stumbling over your words or raising your hand) is often forgotten by others in seconds.

How It Affects You

As a student, the spotlight effect can hold you back by making you:

- **Avoid raising your hand**: You worry about looking "stupid" if you get the answer wrong.
- **Skip asking for help**: You're afraid others will judge you for needing support.
- **Avoid trying new things**: Whether it's joining a club or sharing an idea, you might think all eyes are on you.

The result? You miss out on opportunities to learn, grow, and connect with others, all because of a **misconception** about how much people notice you.

How to Overcome the Spotlight Effect

1. **Remind Yourself: People Are Focused on Themselves**

- Ask yourself: *"What was the last embarrassing thing someone else did?"*
- If you can't remember, it's because you weren't paying attention, and the same applies to others!

2. **Shift Your Focus**

- Instead of worrying about how you look or sound, focus on what **you're trying to accomplish**.
- Example: If you're afraid to ask a question in class, focus on **getting the help you need** instead of what others might think.

3. **Challenge Your Thoughts**

- When you feel like everyone is watching you, ask:
  - *"Is this really true, or am I just imagining it?"*
  - *"Will anyone still care about this tomorrow? Probably not."*

4. **Take Small Steps**

- Start by doing little things that make you uncomfortable, like speaking up in a group or trying something new.
- You'll quickly realize that no one's paying as much attention as you thought.

5. **Be Kind to Yourself**

- Even if someone *does* notice, it's okay! Everyone makes mistakes, has awkward moments, or does things they're unsure about.

Overconfidence Bias

Overconfidence bias happens when you think you've got every-thing under control, but in reality, you're **less prepared than you be-lieve**. It's like convincing yourself you're ready for a test when you've only skimmed the material, only to be blindsided by disappointing re-sults.

How It Shows Up for Students

- **Underestimating how much time you need**: You think study-ing will only take 30 minutes, but you end up feeling over-whelmed when it's harder than expected.
- **Skipping preparation**: You assume you'll "figure it out" during the test or assignment instead of putting in the work beforehand.
- **Avoiding help**: Overconfidence can stop you from asking for support because you believe you've got it covered.

While confidence is **important**, overconfidence tricks you into thinking you're ready when you're not.

How Overconfidence Holds You Back

1. **Poor Results**

   ◦ You overestimate your abilities and **underprepare**, which leads to disappointing outcomes.

2. **Missed Opportunities to Learn**

   ◦ When you assume you know everything, you're less likely to review your work or ask for feedback, two key steps in improving.

3.   **Unnecessary Stress**

  ◦ Overconfidence sets you up for surprises. Realizing you weren't as prepared as you thought can feel overwhelming and discouraging.

How to Avoid Overconfidence Bias

1.   **Test Yourself**

  ◦ Instead of assuming you know the material, **quiz yourself** to check your understanding. If you can't explain it clearly or get stuck, you'll know where to focus.

2.   **Make a Realistic Plan**

  ◦ Break tasks into smaller steps and estimate how much time they'll take, then add extra time as a buffer. This helps you avoid underestimating the effort needed.

3.   **Ask for Feedback**

  ◦ Get input from teachers, friends, or tutors on your work or study habits. **An outside perspective** can help you spot gaps you might have missed.

4.   **Double-Check Your Work**

  ◦ After studying or completing an assignment, take a moment to review it critically. Ask yourself:
    ▪ *"Did I cover everything?"*

- *"What areas still feel unclear?"*

5.   **Stay Humble and Curious**

    ◦ Confidence is great, but balance it with curiosity. Approach learning with the mindset: *"What else can I improve?"*

Availability Heuristic

The **availability heuristic** happens when your brain overestimates the likelihood of something happening just because it's **easily remembered** or fresh in your mind.

For example:

- If you failed a test recently, you might think: *"I'm just going to fail every test."*
- Even though you've studied harder this time, that one failure sticks out, and it **feels** like it will happen again.

How It Affects Students

1. **Messes With Your Confidence**

   ° A single bad experience can make you doubt yourself, even when you've improved or prepared better.

2. **Creates Unnecessary Anxiety**

   ° You start to expect the worst just because it happened before, which can make you more stressed and less focused.

3. **Holds You Back**

   ° If you let one failure define you, you might avoid trying again or give up before you've even started.

How to Overcome the Availability Heuristic

1. **Focus on Facts, Not Feelings**

   - Challenge your thinking by asking:
     - *"Is it true that I always fail tests?"*
     - *"What evidence do I have that I'm better prepared this time?"*
   - Write down your progress: What new steps have you taken to improve?

2. **Look at the Bigger Picture**

   - One bad test or assignment doesn't define your abilities. Think of your **long-term progress**, not just one moment.
   - Example: *"Yeah, I failed that test, but I've done well on other assignments, and I'm working harder now."*

3. **Remind Yourself of Successes**

   - Take a moment to reflect on what you've done well in the past, no matter how small.
   - Success isn't erased by one setback, it's built on trying again.

4. **Focus on What You Can Control**

   - You can't change the past, but you **can control your effort now**.
   - Example: *"I bombed that test last time, but today I'm going to focus on what I know and take it one question at a time."*

5. **Reframe Negative Thoughts**

- Replace thoughts like, *"I'm just going to fail again"* with:
  - *"That was one moment; this time is different."*
  - *"I'm more prepared, and I'm learning from my mistakes."*

Bandwagon Effect

The **bandwagon effect** happens when you do something just because everyone else is doing it. It's like hopping on a moving bandwagon: you go along with the crowd, even if it's not what's best for *you*.

How It Affects Students

1. **Peer Pressure**

   ○ You might follow trends, join activities, or make choices because your friends are doing it, even if it doesn't match your values or goals.
   ○ Example: Everyone's skipping homework to hang out, so you join in, even though you know it'll hurt your grades.

2. **Losing Focus on Your Priorities**

   ○ Following the crowd can distract you from your goals and what *you* want to achieve.

3. **Ignoring What Works for You**

   ○ What's right for others may not be right for you. If you're always copying someone else's path, you might miss out on opportunities that fit you better.

How to Avoid the Bandwagon Effect

1. **Pause and Reflect**

   ○ When you feel the urge to go with the crowd, ask yourself:

- *"Is this what I really want to do?"*
- *"Does this help me reach my goals, or am I just following along?"*

2. **Stick to Your Values**

  ◦ Get clear on what matters to you—your goals, priorities, and boundaries—and make decisions based on *those*, not what others are doing.
  ◦ Example: *"I want to improve my grades, so I'll study tonight instead of going out."*

3. **Be Comfortable Standing Out**

  ◦ It's okay to be different! Standing out can be hard, but it also means you're staying true to yourself.
  ◦ Remind yourself: *"I'm not falling behind; I'm staying on my path."*

4. **Find Supportive Friends**

  ◦ Surround yourself with people who respect your decisions and encourage you to stick to your priorities.

5. **Think Long-Term**

  ◦ Ask yourself: *"Will this decision help me in the long run, or is it just about fitting in right now?"*

Anchoring Bias

Anchoring bias happens when you rely too much on the **first piece of information** you hear and use it as a reference point for everything else.

For example:

- Someone tells you a subject is *super hard*, so you walk into class expecting to struggle, even before you've given it a fair try.
- You hear a teacher is *really strict*, so you're already nervous and disengaged before you meet them.

These first impressions, true or not ,can shape your mindset and influence your performance.

How Anchoring Bias Hurts Students

1. **Creates a Negative Mindset**

    ○ If you go in expecting failure or difficulty, you're less likely to try your best or enjoy the experience.

2. **Stops You From Engaging**

    ○ Anchoring to someone else's opinion can make you give up before you start. You might think:
      - *"What's the point of trying if this is so hard?"*

3. **Limits Your Opportunities**

    ○ Anchoring bias can stop you from discovering that:

- The subject you thought was "impossible" might actually be interesting.
- The "strict" teacher might turn out to be supportive and helpful.

How to Overcome Anchoring Bias

1. **Challenge First Impressions**

   ○ Remind yourself: *"Just because I heard this doesn't mean it's true for me."*
   ○ Be curious and open to forming your own opinion based on your experience.

2. **Focus on What You Can Control**

   ○ Instead of worrying about rumors or expectations, ask yourself:
     - *"What can I do to make this easier for myself?"*
     - *"How can I give this a fair shot?"*

3. **Collect Your Own Evidence**

   ○ Give the class, teacher, or subject a chance before deciding it's too hard or not for you.
   ○ Example: *"I'll focus on learning one thing today and see how I feel after."*

4. **Stay Positive but Realistic**

   ○ Go in with a balanced mindset: *"This might be challenging, but I'll take it step by step and see how it goes."*

Negativity Bias

Negativity bias is when your brain gives way more attention to negative experiences or feedback than positive ones. It's like that one bad moment becomes a spotlight, overshadowing everything good you've done.

For example:

- You get 9 questions right on a test, but you can't stop thinking about the **one you got wrong**.
- A teacher gives you a small piece of criticism, and you forget the praise they gave earlier.

While it's natural to notice negatives, letting them take over can mess with your **confidence, motivation, and self-esteem**.

How Negativity Bias Hurts Students

1. **Kills Your Confidence**

   - When you focus only on what went wrong, you start believing you're not good enough—ignoring your actual progress and successes.

2. **Zaps Motivation**

   - Thinking only about the negatives makes you feel like *"Why even bother?"*, which can stop you from trying.

3. **Hides Your Strengths**

○ You overlook what you're good at because you're too focused on mistakes or bad feedback.

How to Overcome Negativity Bias

1. **Actively Look for the Positives**

   ○ After a tough situation, write down **three things that went well**, no matter how small.
   ○ Example: *"I made a mistake in my essay, but I also wrote a strong introduction and turned it in on time."*

2. **Reframe Negative Thoughts**

   ○ Challenge your thinking:

     ▪ *"Is this one mistake really the whole story?"*
     ▪ *"What did I learn from this that will help me next time?"*

   ○ Instead of *"I got a bad grade, I'm terrible,"* try:

     ▪ *"This grade shows where I can improve, and I'll do better next time."*

3. **Keep a Success Log**

   ○ Write down your **wins and compliments,** no matter how small.
   ○ On bad days, look back at this list to remind yourself of your progress and strengths.

4. **Balance the Scale**

- For every negative thought, challenge yourself to find **two positive ones**.
- Example: *"I missed a question, but I got most of them right, and I studied hard for this."*

5. **Talk to Someone**

- If you're feeling stuck in negativity, talk to a friend, teacher, or mentor who can help you see the bigger picture.

False Consensus Effect

The **false consensus effect** happens when you assume that **everyone else thinks, feels, or experiences things the same way you do**. For example:

- You struggle with a subject but believe *"Everyone else finds this easy, what's wrong with me?"*
- You assume others are naturally better at something, so you feel like you're the only one who can't keep up.

This assumption can make you feel **isolated**, inadequate, or even embarrassed about your struggles.

How It Affects Students

1. **Feelings of Isolation**

    ◦ You start believing you're the "odd one out," which can make you feel alone in your challenges.

2. **Lower Confidence**

    ◦ Thinking you're the only one struggling makes you doubt yourself and feel like you're falling behind.

3. **Missed Support**

    ◦ You might avoid asking for help because you assume no one else needs it.

The Truth: You're Not Alone

Here's the reality:

- **Most people are just doing their best**, they might look confident, but they have their struggles too.
- Everyone learns at their own pace. Just because someone seems to find something easy doesn't mean they actually do.
- Struggling with a subject or task is **normal**, it's part of the learning process.

How to Overcome the False Consensus Effect

1. **Talk to Others**

    - Open up to classmates, friends, or teachers about what you're finding challenging. You'll probably hear:
      - *"Oh, me too!"* or
      - *"I didn't get that either until I asked for help."*

2. **Remind Yourself: Appearances Can Be Misleading**

    - People often hide their struggles, so don't assume that everyone else has it all figured out.

3. **Focus on Your Own Progress**

    - Instead of comparing yourself to what you *think* others are experiencing, track your own growth and effort.

4. **Ask for Help**

○ If you're struggling, **reach out**—teachers, tutors, or peers are there to help. You're not weak for needing support; it's a sign of strength.

5. **Challenge Your Assumptions**

○ Ask yourself: *"Do I really know that everyone finds this easy, or am I just assuming it?"*
○ The answer is usually *no!*

TL;DR: Cognitive Biases That Can Affect Students

1. **Confirmation Bias**: You only notice what supports your beliefs and ignore the rest. If you think you're bad at something, you focus on failures and dismiss successes.
2. **Fixed Mindset**: Believing your abilities can't change makes you avoid challenges and fear failure instead of seeing them as opportunities to grow.
3. **Self-Serving Bias**: Taking credit for successes but blaming failures on outside factors. It stops you from learning and improving.
4. **Sunk Cost Fallacy**: Sticking with something that isn't working because you've already invested time or energy. Sometimes it's better to move on.
5. **Spotlight Effect**: Thinking everyone's paying attention to you when, really, they're focused on themselves. Don't let this stop you from trying.
6. **Overconfidence Bias**: Assuming you're more prepared than you are, which can lead to underpreparation and disappointment.
7. **Availability Heuristic**: Overestimating something's likelihood because it's fresh in your mind. One failure doesn't mean it will happen again.
8. **Bandwagon Effect**: Doing something because "everyone else is," even if it's not right for you. Stick to your own values and goals.
9. **Anchoring Bias**: Relying too much on the first information you hear. Don't let first impressions dictate your experience.
10. **Negativity Bias**: Focusing more on negative experiences than positive ones. Celebrate your wins and remember your strengths.
11. **False Consensus Effect**: Believing everyone feels or thinks the same as you. You're not alone—most people face struggles, even if they don't show it.

Understanding these biases helps you recognize when they're holding you back and make better, more balanced decisions. By challenging these patterns, you can boost your confidence, motivation, and ability to grow!

Foot-in-the-Door Phenomenon: How Small Exceptions Can Derail Big Plans

This principle says that agreeing to a **small request** makes it easier to agree to a **bigger one later**. It's like climbing a "yes" ladder: once you take the first step, it's harder to stop.

For ADHD students, this often shows up as:

- **"Skipping one small task is no big deal, right?"**
- But that small "yes" to skipping creates a pattern, making it easier to skip bigger tasks later.

How It Leads to Procrastination

1. **Starts Small**: You skip a quick review session or push back a minor assignment.
2. **Becomes a Pattern**: It's easier to justify skipping something else because "you already skipped one thing."
3. **Derails the Plan**: Over time, these exceptions snowball, and your entire study or productivity plan might fall apart.

It's a slippery slope that starts with one small decision but can have **big consequences**.

How to Avoid This Trap

1. **Catch Yourself Early**

   ○ Notice when you're tempted to make a small exception. Ask yourself:
      ▪ *"Is this really no big deal, or could it lead to a bigger pattern?"*

2. **Commit to Small Wins**

   ○ Instead of skipping, do a tiny version of the task.
      ▪ Example: If you feel like skipping a 30-minute study session, try doing just 5 minutes instead. A small "win" keeps you on track.

3. **Remind Yourself of the Big Picture**

   ○ Skipping one task feels small now, but it can impact your goals later.
   ○ Repeat: *"Small steps forward add up. Small steps backward do too."*

4. **Make Rules for Yourself**

   ○ Set simple, clear boundaries like:
      ▪ *"If I feel like skipping, I'll do a shorter version of the task instead."*

5. **Track Your Progress**

○ Use a checklist or planner to see how far you've come. Small successes can keep you motivated and help you avoid slipping into exceptions.

TL;DR:

- **What it is**: Saying yes to something small makes it easier to say yes to bigger things later. For ADHD students, this can mean skipping one small task leads to skipping more and more.
- **How it holds you back**: Small exceptions snowball into procrastination, eventually derailing your entire plan.
- **How to avoid it**:
  1. Catch yourself when you're tempted to skip.
  2. Commit to small wins (do 5 minutes instead of skipping entirely).
  3. Keep the big picture in mind: small steps matter.
  4. Set rules to hold yourself accountable.
  5. Track your progress to stay motivated.

Small choices add up, don't let one small exception turn into a habit. A little effort now keeps you on track for the big goals ahead!

28

MOTIVATION AND PROCRASTINATION

What Is Motivation?
Many people think motivation is about having the **energy** or **willpower** to get things done. But that's not exactly true.

Motivation is the reason behind why you do something. It's the **"why"** that gives your actions meaning and direction.

Motivation vs. Energy

Think of it like driving a car:

- **Motivation = Your destination** (where you're going and why you want to get there).
- **Energy/Interest = The fuel** (what keeps you moving).

Even if you know your destination, you won't get anywhere without fuel. But on the flip side, if you don't know **why you're going**, it's hard to find the energy to move at all.

Why Does This Matter for Students?

If you say, *"I don't have motivation,"* you might actually mean:

- You don't see a **clear purpose** in what you're doing.
- You're feeling drained of the **energy** needed to move forward.

Without a strong **"why"**, it's much harder to fuel yourself to keep going, even when the task feels boring, hard, or overwhelming.

How to Boost Your Motivation

1. **Find Your Why**

   ◦ Ask yourself:
      ▪ *"Why am I doing this? How does it help me?"*
      ▪ Example: *"I'm studying because I want to pass this course and work toward my dream job."*

2. **Set Small, Meaningful Goals**

   ◦ Break big tasks into smaller steps and attach a purpose to each one.
   ◦ Example: *"Finishing this paper will help me build discipline and confidence."*

3. **Reframe Tasks You Don't Enjoy**

   ◦ Connect boring or hard tasks to your bigger purpose.
   ◦ Example: *"This assignment isn't fun, but it's part of reaching my long-term goal."*

4. **Refuel Your Energy**

   ◦ Motivation is great, but you still need energy to act. Take breaks, sleep well, eat properly, and manage stress so you have the fuel to keep moving.

TL;DR:

- **Motivation** is the **reason** behind what you do, it's your destination.
- **Energy** or interest is like the fuel that moves you along the path.
- If you lack motivation, it often means you haven't found your **"why"** yet.
- Without knowing your purpose, it's hard to find the energy to keep going.

Find your "why," refuel your energy, and take small steps toward your destination. The clearer your purpose, the easier it is to stay driven!

What Is Procrastination?

At its core, **procrastination** simply means **delaying or postponing something**. That's it. It's not inherently bad, everyone puts things off until the right moment, like doing laundry or cleaning your room.

The problem? Procrastination gets a bad reputation because people often assume it means you're avoiding something important to do something pointless.

Procrastination and ADHD: Why It's Different

For people with ADHD, procrastination often has more to do with **brain chemistry** than laziness or lack of care. Here's why:

1. **Low Dopamine Levels**

    ◦ Dopamine is the "feel-good" chemical that helps you stay interested, focused, and energized to get things done.
    ◦ Tasks like studying or homework don't give your brain much dopamine, so you lose interest **faster** than someone without ADHD.

2. **Seeking Quick Dopamine Boosts**

    ◦ When you hit that dip in interest, your brain naturally looks for something more rewarding: something that gives you a **quick hit of dopamine**.
    ◦ Activities like watching TV, playing video games, or scrolling social media feel way more exciting and satisfying in the moment.

It's not about being lazy, it's about your brain being wired to seek rewards.

Is Procrastination Always Bad?

Nope! Procrastination isn't inherently harmful. Sometimes, taking a break to do something fun can help you recharge and come back to your task with more energy and focus.

The trick is finding a balance:

- **When it's okay to take a break**: You've worked hard and need to recharge.
- **When it's time to push through**: The task is important, and delaying it will create more stress or problems later.

How to Work With Procrastination

1. **Make Tasks More Rewarding**

    - Break big tasks into smaller, manageable steps. Each small win gives you a little dopamine boost.
    - Reward yourself for completing parts of the task. Example: "When I study for 20 minutes, I'll take a 5-minute game break."

2. **Use the "5-Minute Rule"**

    - Tell yourself you'll work on a task for just 5 minutes. Often, once you get started, it's easier to keep going.

3. **Create External Accountability**

    - Share your goals with a friend, parent, or teacher to stay on track.
    - Use reminders, timers, or apps to keep yourself focused.

4.   **Plan Breaks Ahead of Time**

   ◦ Schedule fun, rewarding activities as part of your day. This way, you're giving yourself structured breaks **without guilt**.

Why We Procrastinate: It's Not About Laziness

Procrastination isn't about being lazy or lacking willpower: it's often about avoiding **unpleasant emotions**.

For example:

- **The task feels overwhelming**: You don't know where to start, so you don't start at all.
- **Fear of failure**: You worry you'll mess up, so it's emotionally more comfortable to delay the task.
- **It's boring or uninteresting**: ADHD brains crave dopamine, so less exciting tasks feel extra tough.
- **It makes you feel "dumb" or frustrated**: Avoiding the task helps dodge those uncomfortable feelings.

Instead of blaming yourself, try asking:

- *"What emotions am I trying to avoid right now?"*
- *"Am I afraid to fail, frustrated, or just really bored?"*

Once you know what's really going on, you can tackle procrastination at its root.

What About Active Procrastination?

Procrastination isn't always a total waste of time! There's something called **active procrastination**, where you avoid one task but still work on **other productive things**.

For example:

- You skip your homework but clean your room, organize your desk, or finish small tasks you've been avoiding for weeks.
- You're still getting things done, just not in the order you originally planned.

Why This Matters for ADHD

For people with ADHD, procrastination is often tied to **low dopamine levels**. Boring or overwhelming tasks don't give your brain the dopamine it craves, so you naturally look for more rewarding activities (like watching TV or playing games).

The trick is to use **active procrastination** and **momentum** to your advantage:

- If you've cleaned your room or finished other "less important" tasks, you can build on that productivity streak to tackle the bigger task you're avoiding.
- It's all about balance: taking breaks, staying kind to yourself, and **using your energy where it counts**.

How to Manage Procrastination
1.   **Identify the Emotion**

° Ask yourself: *"What's really making me avoid this task? Fear? Boredom? Frustration?"*

2. **Start Small**

   ° Break the task into tiny, manageable steps.
   ° Example: Instead of "write the essay," start with "write the title."

3. **Use Active Procrastination Wisely**

   ° Do other small productive tasks first (cleaning, organizing, etc.) to build momentum.
   ° Then, ride that momentum to return to the bigger task.

4. **Take Breaks When Needed**

   ° Short, planned breaks can recharge your brain so you're ready to focus again.

5. **Focus on Progress, Not Perfection**

   ° It's okay to move slowly, progress is progress.

TL;DR:
- **What it is**: Procrastination is delaying tasks, often to dodge frustration, boredom, or fear of failure.
- **Why it happens**: ADHD brains crave dopamine, so boring or overwhelming tasks feel harder to stick with.
- **Active procrastination**: Even when you avoid one task, you can still get productive things done—like cleaning or organizing.
- **How to handle it**: Recognize what's holding you back, take small steps, and use active procrastination to build momentum.

Procrastination doesn't have to derail you—understand what's behind it, and use it to your advantage. Balance and self-awareness are key!

HOW TO LEARN AND STUDY

We're now diving into the main reason you got this book: how to learn and study effectively with ADHD or ADHD-like challenges.

Learning happens all the time. Your brain naturally records and connects information from your surroundings. But this is **passive learning**; it just happens without effort.

School requires **active learning**, which is different. It's a skill you have to practice. Most people, especially those with ADHD, don't come by it naturally. But the good news? It's a skill anyone can learn.

29

ACTIVE LEARNING

Active learning is a way of learning that keeps your brain **engaged** and **involved** in the process. Instead of passively trying to absorb information, you're actively doing things to understand, process, and remember it.

For ADHD students, this is a game-changer because:

- Sitting still and listening to a lecture for hours feels like **torture**: your brain craves stimulation.
- Active learning gives your brain the engagement it needs to stay focused and actually make the information stick.

Why Active Learning Works for ADHD

ADHD brains aren't built for passive learning, like listening to long lectures.

- **Too much unengaging information** feels overwhelming, and your brain just **tunes out.**
- Active learning fits how your brain works by keeping it stimulated, helping you stay interested and focused.

Learning vs. Knowing by Heart

In school, there's a lot of emphasis on **memorizing** things, but **learning** and **memorizing** aren't the same.

When you **learn**, you're actually understanding. You know **why** something works, **how** it connects to other ideas, and how to use it in real life. It's like solving a puzzle: your brain creates **connections** that make the information stick and become part of what you already know.

Memorizing, however, is just about storing facts temporarily. You might remember them long enough to pass a test, but they're not meaningful, and they're easily forgotten. It's like copying something into a notebook but never opening it again: it doesn't truly stay with you.

For those with **ADHD**, this is especially tricky. **Short-term memory** is limited, so when you try to memorize, new information often **bumps out the old.** No matter how many times you read your textbook, the facts don't stick because they aren't connected to what you already understand.

The key to lasting knowledge is **learning**. When you learn, you can explain the material, use it in real-life situations, and **build on it** later. **Memorizing** might get you through a test, but **learning** equips you for success far beyond school.

Learning vs. Being Taught

In school, we're **taught** things, but being taught and **learning** aren't the same.

When you're being **taught**, someone else, like a teacher or parent, is giving you information. It's **passive**. They guide you, explain things, and provide instructions. Being taught is important because it gives you the tools and knowledge to start with. But just because you've been taught doesn't mean you've actually **learned**.

Learning is **active**. It's when you take what you've been taught and make sense of it yourself. Learning happens when you practice, experiment, or apply the information. It's when you truly **understand** it, not just because someone told you, but because you've worked through it and made it your own.

For example:

- You might be taught how to solve a math problem, but you've only **learned** it when you can do it on your own and explain why each step works.

Why This Matters

School is designed to teach you, but it doesn't always help you actively learn. It's up to you to figure out **how to learn**, to take what you're taught and turn it into something you really understand and can use.

TL;DR

Being taught is passive: it's when someone gives you information. **Learning** is active: it's when you take that information, process it, and make it your own. Schools often focus on teaching, but real learning happens when you practice and actively engage with what you're taught. For ADHD brains, finding ways to actively learn is key to making the information stick.

What Is Active Learning?

A ctive learning is when you **actively participate** in the process of understanding, processing, and retaining information. It's not about sitting passively while someone teaches you, it's about **engaging with the material** and making it your own.

How Active Learning Works

When you're learning actively, you're doing things like:

- **Asking questions** to clarify and deepen your understanding.
- **Practicing** problems or applying what you've learned.
- **Connecting concepts** to things you already know.
- **Teaching others**, which forces you to really know the material.

This kind of involvement helps your brain:

1. **Understand the bigger picture** instead of just memorizing random facts.
2. **Build stronger connections** between ideas so the information sticks.
3. Stay **engaged** and focused, avoiding the boredom that leads to zoning out.

Why Passive Learning Falls Short

When you're just listening to a lecture or skimming a textbook, your brain isn't doing much. It's like watching letters float by without forming words. It's **hard to remember and even harder to use later**.

ADHD brains especially struggle with this because they're wired to focus on action and stimulation. Sitting still, silently "absorbing" information, often leads to distraction and frustration.

One way of being active in your learning is by using the See one, Do one, Teach one method.

See One, Do One, Teach One

The **"See One, Do One, Teach One"** method is a powerful way to move from simply memorizing to truly **understanding** and retaining information.

How It Works

1. **See One**

   ◦ Start by observing how something is done.
   ◦ This could mean watching a teacher explain a concept, following along with a math problem, or viewing a YouTube tutorial.

2. **Do One**

   ◦ Next, try it yourself.
   ◦ Practice what you just saw: whether it's solving a problem, building something, or completing an example task. This

step helps you apply what you observed and start building confidence.

3.   **Teach One**

- ◦ Finally, explain the concept to someone else.
- ◦ Teaching forces your brain to **organize and process** the information at a deeper level. It also helps you spot any gaps in your understanding and solidifies what you've learned.

This method engages your brain on multiple levels:

- **Seeing** introduces the concept.
- **Doing** strengthens your ability to apply it.
- **Teaching** ensures you've truly mastered the material by putting it into your own words.

Self-Discipline and Active Learning

Active learning takes **self-discipline**. It's about making conscious choices to engage with the material instead of sitting back and hoping it sticks. The payoff? Once you truly **learn** something, it's unlikely you'll forget it.

Why Do You Forget Some Things but Not Others?

It all comes down to **where the information is stored**:

- **Short-Term Memory**: This is where crammed facts live. If you study for a test the night before, the info hasn't had time to stick. Stress or distractions can easily wipe it out.
- **Long-Term Memory**: When you actively learn, your brain creates **connections** that store the information permanently. Once it's in long-term memory, you don't need to "remember" it, it's just there, ready to use.

How Active Learning Helps

Active learning **moves information** from short-term to long-term memory. By engaging with the material, practicing, discussing, and applying it, you build the mental connections needed to lock it in.

It's like **leveling up in a video game**: the more you interact with the content, the stronger and more permanent your understanding becomes.

It Has to Make Sense

The best way to turn **short-term memory** into **long-term knowledge** is by making sense of what you're learning. When you connect new information to something you already know or understand the bigger picture, it sticks better and longer.

Why Random Facts Don't Stick

Your brain hates chaos. Trying to remember a string of ten random digits feels impossible because there's no **pattern** or **context** to anchor it. But as soon as you spot a pattern or link the numbers to something familiar, it becomes much easier to recall, even years later.

This applies to everything you learn. **Straight-up memorizing** random facts without understanding or connecting them won't work in the long run. If it doesn't make sense, your brain won't bother keeping it.

How to Make It Stick

- **Find Patterns**: Look for relationships or connections in what you're learning.
- **Link New Info to What You Know**: Relating new material to something familiar helps your brain create stronger connections.
- **Reflect**: Take time to process and think about the information to help it sink in.

If It Doesn't Make Sense, It's Not Really Learned

Learning happens when things **click** and feel meaningful. If the material doesn't make sense or you don't care about it, memorization is just a short-term fix, it won't stick.

Study and Sleep

Did you know that you **learn better before going to sleep** than in the morning? Sleep is like a personal assistant for your brain, it processes what you've learned during the day and locks it into **long-term memory**.

On the flip side, **lack of sleep** messes up this process. Sleep deprivation makes it much harder for your brain to store information effectively, leaving you frustrated and forgetful. If you're serious about learning, getting enough sleep is just as important as the time you spend studying.

TL;DR

- **Active learning** means getting involved, don't just sit back and hope the info sticks.
- **Patterns and connections** make learning easier, not random memorization.
- Use the **"See one, do one, teach one"** method: Watch, try, and teach to solidify your understanding.
- **Self-discipline** helps move info from short-term to long-term memory.
- **Sleep is critical for learning**, study before bed, and don't skip on rest!

How to Be Active in Your Learning

B eing **active** in your learning means taking steps to engage with the material rather than just passively re-reading or listening. Here are ways to play an active role:

1. Take Notes

- Focus on writing down **important information** during class, not everything the teacher says.
  - Knowing what's important during a lesson can feel overwhelming, but there are strategies to help you identify the key points your teacher is making. Here's how to figure out what really matters:

  ### 1. Listen for Repetition

  - If your teacher repeats something multiple times, it's likely important. Pay attention to phrases like:
    - "This is crucial to remember..."
    - "You'll see this again..."

  ### 2. Watch for Emphasis

  - Teachers often emphasize key points with their tone or body language. Look out for when they:
    - Pause or slow down while explaining.
    - Write something on the board or highlight it on a slide.

3. Follow the Lesson Structure

- Many lessons follow a clear structure. Focus on:
    - **Headings or titles** of sections in presentations.
    - Examples your teacher spends extra time explaining.
    - Summaries or reviews at the end of the class.

4. Pay Attention to Questions

- If your teacher asks a question, the answer is probably important.
- Note questions they say might appear on quizzes or tests.

5. Connect to the Bigger Picture

- Ask yourself:
    - *"How does this information fit into what we've been learning?"*
    - *"Will this help me solve a problem, write an essay, or understand a concept better?"*

6. Ask for Clarification

- If you're unsure what's important, don't hesitate to ask:
    - "Is this something we should focus on for the test?"
    - "Can you explain how this fits into the main topic?"

- Even jotting down **titles or key points** from PowerPoints can help keep you focused.
- Your notes will give you a roadmap for what to study later.

2. Ask Questions

- If you don't understand something, **ask for an explanation**.
- If you're uncomfortable speaking up in class, wait until after or schedule a meeting with your teacher.
- Not every teacher will be flexible, but it's still worth trying.

3. Make Your Own Research

- Use the internet to **find additional explanations**:
  - Ask Google or ChatGPT to simplify a concept.
  - Explore forums like Reddit where people can share their knowledge.
- Your smartphone or computer is a **powerful tool**, use it to your advantage!

4. Engage Your Senses

- The more **senses** you involve, the better you'll remember. For example:
  - **Reading** engages your eyes.
  - **Writing or drawing** engages touch.
  - **Talking aloud** engages your hearing.
- Be creative, find ways to involve multiple senses to make learning stick.

5. Rewrite Your Notes in Your Own Words

Your notes should make sense to **you**. After class, take some time to rewrite them using words and explanations you'd use to explain the material to someone else. This helps solidify your understanding and ensures the information is more relatable to your brain.

6. Teach It

This is one of the best ways to learn and identify gaps in your understanding. At the end of the day:

- Teach what you've learned to someone at home, a friend online, or even an inanimate object like a plushie.
- Teaching a real person is ideal because they can ask questions that challenge you to dive deeper.
- Re-explaining what you learned helps move the information to **long-term memory** and shows you what you still need to work on.

7. Take Breaks

Don't just reread notes or textbooks repeatedly, it's not effective. When you feel stuck:

- Take a break to let your brain work quietly in the background.
- Sleep on it; your brain will continue processing and recognizing patterns while you rest.
- Return to the problem with a fresh perspective, and the solution may come more easily.

8. Make It Fun

Studying doesn't have to be boring! If you enjoy the process, you're more likely to remember what you've learned.

- Play some music, order a snack, and turn your study session into a mini celebration.
- Positive emotions help your brain form stronger **long-term memories**.

9. Use Your Whole Brain

Learning isn't just about logic, it's about engaging both sides of your brain.

- **Draw pictures and diagrams** to engage your creative side.
- Pair visuals with logical sequences to strengthen understanding.
- Try building small demos or acting out the problem with your hands. This physical engagement makes the material stick better.

10. Avoid Memorization

Instead of cramming random facts or formulas, focus on **understanding the concepts** and learning how to solve problems. Memorization only works in the short term, and it's much less effective if you don't understand what you're trying to remember. When you understand, things stick naturally.

11. Learn from Your Mistakes

Mistakes aren't failures, they're some of your best teachers. When you get a test back, don't just look at your grade.

- **Study your mistakes**: What went wrong, and why?
- Revisit the concepts you didn't understand, and work through them again.

Mistakes show you what needs more attention. They teach you to approach problems differently and deepen your understanding.

If you're not making mistakes, you're not challenging yourself enough. School isn't about being perfect; it's about learning through **trial and error**.

12.Find a System That Works for You

Forget the one-size-fits-all study tips. If studying in silence helps you focus, go for it. But if background noise or a little distraction keeps you stimulated, that's fine too.

Some people need to focus on one task at a time, while others thrive when juggling multiple assignments. ADHD brains are unique, so the **right system is the one that works for you**.

TL;DR

- **Avoid memorization**: Focus on understanding, not cramming facts.
- **Learn from mistakes**: They're opportunities to grow, not failures. Use them to improve your approach and deepen your knowledge.
- **Find your system**: Study how it works for you—whether it's silence, noise, one task at a time, or switching between tasks.

Make learning your own. Engage with it, embrace mistakes, and discover what works best for you!

30

GETTING IN ACTION

A ctive learning is fantastic, but none of it works if you can't get started on your homework or studies. The hardest part is often just **getting into motion**, and that's where the **Big Rock Analogy** can help.

The Big Rock Analogy

I magine you're standing next to a **huge round rock,** about three feet wide. Your task is to move this rock from **Point A to Point B**.

The problem? The rock doesn't move on its own. It's sitting there, resisting change, just like you when you're stuck on the couch avoiding your homework.

This is called **inertia**: objects (and people) resist changes in their motion. The hardest part of moving the rock is that **first push**. But once it starts rolling, it takes way less effort to keep it going.

What This Means for You

Getting started on a task, whether it's studying, cleaning, or anything else, feels like that **big first push**. It's the hardest part because your brain is resisting change. But once you're in motion, it's easier to keep going.

The trick is to focus on **that one first push**, not the whole journey.

ADHD-Friendly Tips to Get in Action

The Big Rock Analogy in Practice

Getting started is the hardest part. You have to be the one to make the **first push**, or nothing will happen. The good news? It's a skill you can practice, and it gets easier over time. If one trick doesn't work, don't stress, you're not the problem. Try again or try a different approach.

Tip 1: Just Pick Something

Ever spent forever scrolling Netflix or staring at your to-do list, waiting for something to *feel right*? That's decision paralysis: it happens when you're scared of making the "wrong" choice.

Here's the trick: **just pick something** and start.

- If it's the wrong choice, it's fine! You can always switch.
- Testing things out saves you time in the long run because it helps you figure out what works and what doesn't. You might take 5 minutes to realize it's not what you wanted instead of spending 45 minutes finding the right thing to do, but not trying anything.

Starting down a path you don't finish isn't failure. It's **progress**, and that's what matters.

TL;DR

Getting started is hard, but it's a skill you can build. Don't wait for the "perfect" choice. **Pick something and start,** even if it's not the right fit, switching is faster than staying stuck in indecision. The key is to move forward!

Tip 2: Create Momentum

If you're anything like me, when there's a big task looming, you might find yourself tackling a bunch of small, unrelated tasks instead. That's not always a bad thing! This is called **active procrastination,** as we seen it earlier, and you can use it to your advantage.

Every small task you finish creates a sense of **momentum**: a string of little victories that can shift you into an active, productive mindset. The key is to **acknowledge and appreciate those small wins**. Be proud of yourself, not for avoiding the big task, but for knocking out all those smaller tasks that needed attention too.

This sense of accomplishment and competence helps make the big task less intimidating. Plus, since you're already in motion, the effort required to start the bigger job feels much smaller than it did before.

TL;DR

Turn active procrastination into a tool. Completing small tasks builds momentum and confidence, making it easier to tackle the big task. Celebrate the small victories, and you'll find the big one feels far less overwhelming.

Tip 3: If It's Worth Doing, It's Worth Doing Badly

Half-assing something is **better than not doing it at all**. Even if you're not doing it perfectly, **finishing** is a win. Just getting 1% done is better than 0%.

The key is to **start**. Fear of imperfection can keep you from beginning, but here's the thing:

- You can always improve things later.

• Progress, no matter how small, is still progress.

Perfection Isn't Required

Let's say you're skimming a text and only grasp 30% of the information. That's still better than spending forever on the first paragraph hoping to understand it perfectly. Just **get through it**, and you can always revisit it later for more details.

Doing things imperfectly doesn't mean you're lazy or incompetent; it means you're working through the process. Over time, you'll improve.

Celebrate Small Wins

Stop comparing yourself to unrealistic expectations. Instead:

- If you wash three plates when you thought you'd do none—that's a win.
- If you clear a tiny corner of your desk, instead of the whole thing—that's progress.
- If you answer three homework questions when you were planning to do nothing—that's success.

Every little bit counts.

TL;DR
Don't aim for perfect—just doing **something** is better than doing nothing. Finishing, even imperfectly, is a win. Celebrate small victories, focus on progress over perfection, and remember that starting imperfectly is still starting.

Tip 4: The Final Countdown

A Simple Trick to Get Moving

When you're feeling stuck and can't get yourself to start, try this:

- **Countdown from 5 to 0** in your head or out loud.
- Once you hit 0, **immediately take the first step**.

For example:

- Countdown, and then just **stand up**.
- Countdown, and then **open your textbook**.

You don't have to commit to finishing the entire task. The goal is to just **start**, that first push makes all the difference.

The countdown gives your brain a clear signal to stop overthinking and take action. By focusing on one **tiny, manageable step**, you reduce the overwhelm of the bigger task. Once you've made the first move, it's easier to keep going—you've already beaten inertia.

TL;DR

Stuck? Countdown from 5 to 0, then take the first step, like standing up or opening your book. It's a simple brain hack to stop overthinking and start moving. Once you're in motion, it's easier to keep going.

Tip 5: The Green Zone

What Is the Green Zone?

The **green zone** is the time of day when you feel most energized, focused, and productive. For some, it's early in the morning, for others, it might be late at night or somewhere in between.

This is when your brain and body are **in sync**, so it's the best time to tackle your most important or demanding tasks.

Other Energy Zones

- **Yellow Zone**: When you feel a bit sluggish (like after lunch) but still have some energy. Use this time for lighter, less demanding tasks.
- **Red Zone**: When your energy is completely drained. During this time, focus on **resting or recharging** instead of forcing productivity. It's okay to give yourself permission to rest!

How to Use Your Zones

- **Identify** your green, yellow, and red zones by paying attention to when you feel most alert and when you tend to fade.
- **Plan your day** around your energy flow:
  - Use your **green zone** for tasks that require focus and creativity.
  - Save easier tasks for the **yellow zone**.
  - Rest or recharge during the **red zone** without guilt: it's necessary.

TL;DR

Your **green zone** is when you're at peak energy, use it for important tasks. Save lighter work for your **yellow zone** and rest during your **red**

zone. Working with your natural energy flow makes your day more productive and less stressful.

Tip 6: INCU: Making Tasks ADHD-Friendly

For people with ADHD, tasks are easier to start or finish if they are:

- **Interesting**
- **New**
- **Challenging**
- **Urgent**

If a task doesn't fit into at least one of these categories, it's much harder to get that dopamine rush needed to focus.

How to Use INCU

If a task feels boring or overwhelming, tweak it to fit one of these criteria:

- **Make it interesting**: Turn it into a game or add a reward at the end.
- **Make it new**: Find a fresh angle or approach. For example, study in a new spot or use colorful notes.
- **Make it challenging**: Set mini-goals or time yourself to see how much you can get done.
- **Make it urgent**: Create a deadline or use a timer to add pressure.

These adjustments can make even mundane tasks more engaging and doable.

This explains why you might hyperfocus on things that **excite you** or why you dive headfirst into **new projects**. It's not that you can't focus, it's that the task needs to fit one of these key criteria to feel rewarding

TL;DR

For ADHD, tasks become easier if they're **Interesting, New, Challenging, or Urgent**. Use these criteria to tweak tasks: gamify them, add deadlines, or create mini-goals. It's about working with how your brain naturally works, not forcing it.

Tip 7: 5-Minute Sprint

Sometimes, all you need to get started is just **five minutes**. The idea is simple:

- Set a **5-minute timer** or play **two favorite songs**.
- Sprint through the task during that time.

There's **no pressure to finish**, and that's the point. You're only committing to start and make some progress.

- **It's not intimidating**: Five minutes feels manageable, and it lowers the mental barrier to starting.
- **Momentum builds naturally**: Often, once you start, you'll find it easier to keep going even after the timer ends.
- **Progress adds up**: A few 5-minute sprints throughout the day can lead to an hour or more of productivity.

How to Use It

1. Pick a task.
2. Set a timer for 5 minutes.
3. Start!
4. When the timer goes off, decide: stop or keep going?

No matter what, you'll have done something productive, and that's always a win.

TL;DR
Use a **5-minute timer** or two songs to tackle a task without pressure to finish. The goal is to start and make progress. Quick sprints like this break the barrier of starting and can lead to surprising productivity by the end of the day!

Tip 8: Don't Wait for "Motivation"
We often think motivation is the spark we need to get started, but that's **not how it works**. Motivation doesn't come first; it **follows action**.

When you start doing something, even something small, it triggers feelings of accomplishment. That releases **dopamine**, the reward chemical in your brain. Dopamine gives you the boost to keep going, creating a positive cycle: **action → dopamine → more action**.

How to Trigger Motivation

- Start small: Get out of bed, finish a paragraph, or do one simple task.
- **Celebrate your wins**: Feel proud, even for small accomplishments. This boosts dopamine and keeps you moving forward.
- Avoid negative self-talk: If you shame yourself (e.g., "Ugh, it's about time"), you kill the dopamine reward. Instead, acknowledge the effort and be kind to yourself.

Remember

Tasks don't have to feel fun or exciting to be done. Use small actions to kickstart the dopamine cycle. The more wins you rack up, no matter how small, the easier it becomes to tackle bigger tasks.

TL;DR

Don't wait for motivation. Take **action first**, even if it's small. Action triggers dopamine, which makes you feel good and motivates you to do more. Celebrate your victories (big or small), and keep the cycle going. Motivation comes after action, not before.

Tip9: If Being Hard on Yourself Worked… It Would Have by Now

You've probably spent years being harsh on yourself because that's what you were taught. Growing up in a world built for neurotypical people, you've felt like you weren't enough. That criticism, both from others and yourself, became a habit. But here's the thing: **it hasn't helped.**

Now that you know more about ADHD and how your brain works, you can see it's **not your fault**. Your brain functions differently, and the traditional systems and expectations aren't designed for you. That doesn't make you lazy or incompetent, it just means you need tools that align with your neurotype.

What to Try Instead

Be **gentle with yourself**.

- **Talk to yourself like you would a friend**: You wouldn't call your best friend lazy or dumb, so why do it to yourself?

- Practice **compassion and patience**: Your brain is doing its best, even if it works differently.
- Unlearn harsh habits and give yourself the kindness you deserve.

Criticizing yourself won't magically make things better. But self-compassion can. When you respect and understand your brain, you create space to build systems that actually work for you.

TL;DR

Being hard on yourself doesn't work, so try kindness instead. Your brain works differently, and that's not your fault. Treat yourself like you'd treat a friend: with patience, compassion, and respect. You're doing your best, and that's enough.

Tip 10: Break Down the Steps

For ADHD brains, vague tasks like "write the paper" or "clean the house" are too abstract and overwhelming. Breaking them into **tiny, specific steps** makes them manageable and easier to start.

How to Do It

1. **Go Small... Really Small**

    ◦ Break tasks into the smallest, most tangible actions.
    ◦ Example: Instead of "clean the kitchen," start with "wash one plate."

2. **Focus on One Step at a Time**

    ◦ If the full list feels overwhelming, hide it.
    ◦ Reveal just one step at a time and focus only on that.

3. **Be Specific**

- Replace vague tasks like "write the paper" with actionable steps like:
    - Choose a topic.
    - Find four sources.
    - Write the introduction.

4. **Work Backward**

- Imagine the final step and ask, "What comes right before this?"
- Keep working backward until you reach the starting point.
- This creates a roadmap, making the task feel less daunting.

5. **Celebrate Small Wins**

- Checking off even tiny steps gives a hit of accomplishment and motivation.

TL;DR

For overwhelming tasks, **break them into tiny, specific steps** like "wash one plate" or "write one sentence." Focus on one step at a time, and if the full list feels like too much, hide it. Work backward to create a roadmap if needed. Small steps add up to big accomplishments, and every tiny win fuels your momentum.

Tip 11: Trick Your Brain

Your brain loves patterns, and you can use that to your advantage by **associating specific cues with certain tasks**. These cues act as signals that help your brain switch modes without relying on sheer willpower.

How to Trick Your Brain

- **Music:** Create task-specific playlists (e.g., one for cleaning, one for studying). Playing the same songs every time builds an automatic association.
- **Clothing:** Wear the same shirt, hoodie, or outfit for specific tasks to signal to your brain, "It's time to work."
- **Smells:** Light a particular candle or use a specific scent (e.g., peppermint gum) to cue focus or productivity.
- **Routines:** Add small rituals, like sitting in a specific chair or making a certain type of tea, to create task-ready habits.

Why It Works

These cues create **patterns that your brain recognizes**. Over time, hearing that playlist, smelling that candle, or putting on that shirt automatically gets you in the mood for the task. You can also use this trick for winding down, like creating a bedtime routine that signals your brain it's time to sleep.

TL;DR

Trick your brain into productivity by linking cues, like music, clothes, or smells, to specific tasks. These signals help your brain switch into the right mode automatically, making starting tasks easier without relying on willpower.

Tip 12: Body Double

Sometimes, no matter how many strategies you try, you just **can't start on your own**. When this happens, having a **body double**, someone who sits with you while you tackle a task, can make all the difference.

How a Body Double Helps

- **Physical Presence:** Just having someone nearby can reduce the pressure and help you focus.
- **Accountability:** Knowing someone is there makes it harder to ignore the task.
- **Motivation Boost:** Working with someone else can make tasks feel less daunting and even fun.

It's Okay to Ask for Help

Needing support doesn't mean you're failing. ADHD is a disability, and it's normal to need **extra help**. Asking someone you trust to sit with you, whether they're actively helping or just keeping you company ,can make overwhelming tasks manageable.

TL;DR

Feeling stuck? Ask someone you trust to be your **body double**. Their presence can motivate you, ease the stress, and help you get started. Needing help isn't failure, it's just the nudge you need to push forward.

Tip 13: Surround Yourself with Your Project

When you're excited about a project but can't seem to start, **immerse yourself in the topic**:

- Read articles or books about it.
- Watch YouTube videos.
- Listen to podcasts.
- Write down all the benefits and positive outcomes once it's done.

By surrounding yourself with the subject, you let the **hype build naturally**. Think of it like swimming in excitement until it reaches a point where you can't help but dive in.

A Word of Caution

This method works best when you believe in your ability to complete the project. If consuming content about it makes you feel **inspired**, great! But if it makes you feel discouraged or doubt yourself, it might not be the right time for this approach.

TL;DR

Stuck starting a project? Immerse yourself in the topic, watch, read, and listen to build excitement. Let the hype push you into action, but make sure the process inspires confidence, not self-doubt!

Tip 14: No Energy? No Problem!

If you're feeling drained, don't worry, there are still ways to make progress:

- **Read articles** or class materials on your phone.
- **Watch tutorial videos** to break down tasks into simple steps.
- **Listen to podcasts** for insights and inspiration without lifting a finger.

You don't need to physically engage with a task to start moving toward your goals. Learning and gathering ideas while relaxing can still set the stage for action later.

Even when you're not actively "doing," you're preparing and building a foundation. **Small steps**, like learning from your couch or bed, count just as much toward your progress.

TL;DR

Feeling low energy? Use online resources like videos, podcasts, and articles to gather knowledge and inspiration without leaving your couch. Even small steps can lead to big progress!

31

STAYING IN ACTION

Alright, we started; we did the first step!

How do we stay in action? Let's try these ADHD-friendly tips and triks!

The "Meh, Might as Well" Principle

The "meh, might as well" principle is a simple trick to keep yourself going once you've started something. It's about taking small steps that naturally lead to the next one, making it easier to stay in action.

- **Start Tiny**: Pick one super simple task, like picking up a single shirt or reading the first line of your textbook.
- **Build Momentum**: Once you've started, you can just say "meh, might as well do the next step" to keep going.
  - Pick up another shirt.
  - Read the second line of the textbook.
  - Grab those dirty dishes while you're heading to the kitchen.
- **Think of It Like a Domino Effect**: Each small step makes the next one easier, and before you know it, you've made real progress.

This method works because it reduces the pressure of tackling big tasks. You're not committing to the whole thing: just the **next tiny**

step. Once you're in motion, your brain is more willing to stay in action.

TL;DR

Start with a small, easy task like picking up one shirt or reading one line of your textbook. The "meh, might as well" principle keeps you going step by step, turning tiny actions into real progress without feeling overwhelmed, because once you've done something small, meh, might as well do the next step!

M OVE!

People with ADHD thrive on **novelty** and controlled changes. Shifting your environment can make tasks feel fresh and exciting, breaking the monotony that often kills motivation.

- **Change Your Spot**: Move your work to a new location, like the kitchen, a café, or even outside.
- **Rearrange Your Space**: Try a new layout for your room or workspace. Small changes can make a big impact.
- **Use New Tools**: Switch up your pens, notebooks, or even your digital tools to bring a sense of freshness.
- **Add Novelty**: This taps into the INCU criteria, sparking your brain's interest and helping you stay engaged.

A change of scenery or setup disrupts the habit of not working. It gives your brain a subtle reset, making it easier to start or keep going.

TL;DR

Switch up your workspace or tools to add novelty and break the monotony. A new environment or setup can refresh your focus and make it easier to dive into your tasks.

Pomodoro Method

The **Pomodoro Method** is a time management tool that uses short, focused work sessions followed by regular breaks to help you stay productive.

1. Choose a task.
2. **Work for a set time** (e.g., 10-60 minutes, whatever feels doable for you).
3. Take a **5-minute break:** step away from your workspace, grab a snack, or relax.
4. Repeat the cycle. After four sessions, take a longer **20-minute break**.

Why It Works

- **Short Bursts Reduce Overwhelm**: Focusing for just 15 minutes feels way easier than committing to two hours straight.
- **Built-In Breaks Help Resist Distractions**: Knowing a break is coming soon makes it easier to avoid interruptions.
- **Gamifies Productivity**: Turning work into timed sessions feels like a manageable game.

Tips for ADHD Brains

- Customize the focus time to fit your energy: start with shorter intervals if needed.
- Use a timer or app to track your sessions and breaks.
- Don't feel bad if you need to step away entirely; come back when you're ready.

TL;DR

The Pomodoro Method helps you stay focused with short work sessions (10-60 minutes) followed by 5-minute breaks. After four cycles, take a 20-minute break. It reduces overwhelm, keeps distractions in check, and turns productivity into a game!

Create a Reward System

ADHD brains thrive on **dopamine**, the brain's "feel-good" chemical. Rewards trigger dopamine, making tasks more enjoyable and helping you stay motivated.

How to Use Rewards Effectively

1. **Break Tasks Into Small Steps**

   ◦ Instead of aiming to finish an entire project, reward yourself after smaller wins like writing an introduction or studying for 15 minutes.

2. **Choose Rewards You Love**

   ◦ Pick things you genuinely look forward to, like a favorite snack, watching a YouTube video, or playing a game.

3. **Match the Reward to the Effort**

   ◦ Bigger tasks deserve bigger rewards, but even small tasks can earn tiny rewards to keep you going.

4. **Mix It Up**

   ◦ Keep rewards fresh and exciting. One day it could be chocolate; the next, a quick scroll through social media or a longer break for gaming.

The Goal

The idea is to make tasks less daunting and keep yourself engaged by associating effort with fun, positive outcomes. It's not about bribing yourself, it's about creating a system that works with how your brain is wired.

TL;DR

Use rewards to keep yourself motivated. Break tasks into small steps, set rewards for each win, and choose things you love. Mix up your rewards to keep things exciting, and watch as even boring tasks feel more doable!

Stay Stimulated

For ADHD brains, focus isn't just about removing distractions, it's about finding the **right level of stimulation** to stay engaged. Tasks that feel boring or routine can quickly derail concentration, even in distraction-free spaces.

Strategies to Stay Stimulated

1. **Controlled Distractions**

   ○ Play your favorite music, put on a familiar TV show in the background, or listen to white noise to create a stimulating environment without overwhelming your focus.

2. **Work on Multiple Tasks**

   ○ Switch between projects when you feel bored. For some ADHDers, multitasking can actually keep things exciting and prevent burnout on any single task.

3. **Inject Fun Into Your Routine**

   ○ Take quick breaks for fun activities, like a 5-minute dance party or a walk around the room. These bursts of energy can help reset your focus.

4. **Experiment With Your Environment**

   ○ Some people thrive in clutter-free spaces, while others focus better with a bit of chaos or sensory input. Find what works best for your brain.

Create a balance that keeps your brain stimulated and engaged. Avoid boredom by adding excitement, movement, or novelty to your tasks while keeping distractions under control.

TL;DR
ADHD brains need stimulation to focus. Use music, background noise, or multitasking to stay engaged. Take quick, fun breaks and adjust your environment to suit your needs. It's all about finding what works for you to keep tasks interesting and manageable!

A System That Works is a Good System

The bottom line is **simple**: if a system helps you get things done, then it's a good system for you. There's no one-size-fits-all solution, especially for ADHD brains. What matters is finding what works **for your unique traits** and sticking with it.

Make It Your Own
- **Learn Your Style**: Take time to understand how your brain works and adapt strategies to match.
- **Mix and Match**: Combine tips or modify them to suit your needs. Start with one strategy to get going and switch to another to stay in motion.
- **Experiment**: Try different approaches. The more you test, the closer you'll get to a system that feels natural and effective.

Remember, there's no "wrong way" if it helps you accomplish what you need. Be flexible, be creative, and most importantly—be kind to yourself during the process.

TL;DR
If it works, it's a good system! Take time to learn your unique style, mix and match strategies, and experiment to find the perfect approach. Tailor everything to fit your needs, there's no wrong way if it helps you succeed!

32

ORGANIZATION AND PLANNING

To-Do Lists

One big reason we freeze up is because we don't know where to start or the path to the finish feels blurry. That's where a **to-do list** can be a game-changer, it's your **personal map** to get unstuck.

How to Create a To-Do List

1. **Write Everything Down**: List all the tasks you need to do, big or small.
2. **Break Tasks Into Smaller Steps**: For example, instead of "finish homework," break it into "read chapter 3," "do exercise 1," and "write essay outline."
3. **Prioritize**:

   - Focus on what's **important and urgent** first.
   - Use tools like the **Eisenhower Matrix**:

	IMPORTANT	NOT IMPORTANT
URGENT:	Do it today!	Ask for help/delegate it.
NOT URGENT:	Schedule it.	Do only if you have time.

4.   **Check Off Your Tasks**: Crossing off items gives you a boost of motivation!

What If You Forget to Check Your List?

It's normal at first, it's a habit you'll build over time. Here are ways to make it easier:

- **Bullet Journals**: Add creativity to make it fun.
- **Apps**: Use ones that send reminders.
- **Sticky Notes**: Place them where you'll see them often, like your computer or desk.

Over time, checking your list will become easier. Probable not like a second nature, but easier.

TL;DR

Feeling stuck? Use a to-do list to map out your tasks and break them into smaller, manageable steps. Prioritize important and urgent tasks with tools like the Eisenhower Matrix. Build the habit of checking your list with creative tools like journals, apps, or sticky notes. It'll help you stay on track and feel accomplished!

Visual Reminders

Let's face it, ADHD and memory aren't exactly best friends. Forgetting stuff isn't a flaw; it's just how our brains work. A solution? **Visual reminders** that make your tasks impossible to ignore!

- **Sticky Notes**:

  - Stick them anywhere you'll see them: mirrors, your fridge, your desk.
  - Write short, clear reminders like "Finish math homework" or "Take out the trash."
  - **Refresh Them**: If you stop noticing them (hello, brain blind spots), switch it up with new colors, placements, or designs to make them stand out again.

- **Whiteboards**:

  - Perfect for daily to-do lists, weekly goals, or upcoming deadlines.
  - Place it somewhere visible, like your room or workspace.
  - Use **colors** to make it engaging and satisfying, erasing tasks once they're done feels amazing!

Why It Works

ADHD brains don't always hold onto abstract ideas like "I need to email my teacher later." Visuals make these ideas **concrete** and keep them front and center. Seeing the reminder every day prevents you from forgetting, and it's easier than relying on willpower alone.

TL;DR

ADHD brains thrive with **visual reminders**. Use sticky notes or a whiteboard to keep important tasks front and center. Refresh reminders regularly to keep them noticeable, and don't forget to make them colorful and fun!

Timers and Alarms

Timers and alarms can be a game-changer for staying on track, especially for ADHD brains. Time often feels like a blur, either too fast or too slow, making it hard to manage. But alarms and timers can act as your personal assistant, keeping you grounded and on schedule.

- **Set Alarms for Your Day**:

  - Use alarms to structure your day: wake up, start homework, take a break, or leave for school.
  - Think of them as reminders from "future you" saying, *"Hey, it's time to do the thing!"*

- **Timers for Tasks**:

  - Use timers for focus bursts, like the **Pomodoro method**: 25 minutes of work, followed by a 5-minute break.
  - For starting tasks, set a short 5- or 10-minute timer to ease into it. When the timer ends, switch to your next task.

Overcoming the Snooze Trap

Ignoring alarms is a common problem. To avoid this:

- Use **hard-to-ignore sounds**: a favorite song, an annoying tone, or something energizing.
- Place your alarm **across the room** so you have to physically get up to turn it off.
- **Move immediately** when the alarm rings, even if it's just standing up. This breaks the cycle of staying stuck.

Remember the **Foot-in-the-Door Phenomenon**: starting small helps you keep going.

Why They Work

Timers and alarms provide structure and help you break overwhelming tasks into manageable pieces. By responding consistently, they create a routine that helps ADHD brains thrive.

TL;DR

Alarms and timers are ADHD-friendly tools for managing time. Use alarms to structure your day and timers for short focus bursts (like the Pomodoro method). Avoid snoozing by using energizing sounds, placing alarms out of reach, and moving immediately when they ring. They work best when used consistently!

Your Brain Can't Remember What It Never Learned

Sometimes, it feels like your brain is failing you, like when you can't remember where you put your phone or whether you locked the door. But here's the thing: **your brain can't remember what it never actually learned or registered**.

When you do something without consciously paying attention, your brain doesn't store that information. So, it's not that you forgot; it's more like your brain never recorded it in the first place.

This happens a lot with ADHD brains because focus and attention are already a challenge. If your mind is elsewhere while you're placing your phone down, your brain doesn't register it. It's frustrating, but it's not your fault, it's just how your brain works.

So next time you lose your keys or can't remember if you locked the door, remind yourself: **it's not about forgetting, it's about not noticing in the first place.**

TL;DR

Your brain only remembers what it actually pays attention to. If you can't recall where you put something, it's not that you forgot; your brain might not have registered it at all. This is common with ADHD, so be patient with yourself.

CONCLUSION

We hope this book has helped you gain a better understanding of how your brain works and given you practical ways to trick it, and your environment, to make studying and learning easier.

Living and learning with ADHD can be tough, especially in a society and school system designed for neurotypical brains. But you're not the problem. **You have a disability, and that's okay.** It just means your path will look different, and it might take a bit more work to find what works for you.

The most important takeaway? **There's no one-size-fits-all solution.** What works for someone else might not work for you, and that's perfectly okay. The goal isn't to try to become neurotypical, that's an unrealistic and unnecessary goal. Instead, focus on understanding your unique brain, playing to your strengths, and developing strategies that fit *you*.

Be patient and kind to yourself. Every small step you take, every experiment with a new method, and every tiny victory is a huge accomplishment. It's about progress, not perfection.

Learning is a journey, not a race. Stay resilient, embrace the process, and remember: you can do this. And when you do, you'll look back and be so proud of everything you've achieved.

You've got this!

33

TL;DR

THE BEAUTY OF NEURODIVERSITY

Neurodiversity depicts the vast range of diversity and differences in how the human brain is wired. It is often divided between neurotypicals and "all the others" (neurodivergents).

The brain rules everything we experience, and neurotypical (NT) brains have a different "base code" than neurodivergent (ND) brains, impacting the way all the other connections are created.

Trying to reach neurotypical expectations of life (and they are everywhere) when you are neurodivergent often leads to suffering, confusion, and frustration. There is nothing wrong with ND brains, and society needs to be more inclusive.

EXECUTIVE FUNCTIONS

Executive functions (EFs) are brain processes controlled by the **frontal lobe** that help us **plan, start, and complete tasks.**

School and work systems assume everyone's EFs function the same way, but **this isn't true.**

EFs vary widely, especially between **neurotypical (NT)** and **neuro-divergent (ND)** people.

Each ND person experiences EFs **differently**, and these strengths and challenges can even **change over time.**

- **Deductive reasoning** is the ability to **fill in the blanks** when information is missing.
- Neurotypical (NT) brains do this **subconsciously**, while autistic and ADHD brains often require **clear instructions** to know what's expected.

- For autistic and ADHD people, tasks require **detailed, step-by-step instructions**, especially when the task is new or unfamiliar.
- **Planning and prioritization** involve creating a **mental roadmap** for tasks and ranking them by importance.
- **NT brains** do this **automatically**, while **ND brains** must do it **manually** through conscious effort.
- For ND people, planning takes **time, energy, and familiarity**—and prioritization can be especially tricky because **everything feels equally important.**

- **Organization** is the ability to bring order to our **environment** and **thoughts.**
- It helps us **keep spaces tidy**, remember what we need, and communicate clearly.
- **ND brains** don't organize automatically. This requires **time, energy**, and focus, which can be hard to manage under stress or fatigue.

- **Problem solving** is the ability to adapt to unexpected challenges by **parsing past experiences** or **breaking problems into smaller parts.**

- NT brains handle this **instinctively**, while ND brains must do it **manually**, which takes **time, energy,** and conscious effort.
- ND individuals can build problem-solving skills by having **positive, supportive experiences** with obstacles over time.
- Problem solving is linked to **planning, prioritization, and organization**, making it an everyday challenge for ND people.

- **Working memory** (short-term memory) is the brain's ability to temporarily store information we need in the moment.
- **ADHDers** and many **autistic people** have **fewer memory slots** than NT brains, so they can't store as much short-term information.
- Forgetting happens when the brain **runs out of space** or **never records the information to begin with.**

- ADHD and autistic brains give their attention to the **most stimulating and interesting thing** around.
- Forcing them to persist in a boring or unengaging task is **useless and draining.**
- They need **breaks** and time to recharge their attention through activities that bring **dopamine and stimulation.**
- The ADHD brain is **designed to notice everything**—sounds, thoughts, and changes in the environment.

- Focusing for hours on a boring task is **not natural** for them.
- They need tasks to be **highly interesting or stimulating** to shut out "distractions" and stay focused.

- ADHDers and some autistic people have a **blurry sense of time**, both for the **past** and the **future.**
- **Far-off deadlines** feel intangible, making their brains behave as if they don't exist yet.

- They struggle with knowing when to start tasks or how long they'll take because time feels vague and abstract.
- Long-term goals don't consistently motivate them because they're too far away to feel real.

OBJECT PERMANENCE

- **Out of sight, out of mind:** ADHDers and AuDHDers forget about tasks, objects, ideas, and even people if they're not physically present or immediately visible.
- Forgetting doesn't mean they don't care—it's just how their brains are wired.
- To keep track of ideas or reminders: **Write them down, set an alarm, or tell someone.**
- Object permanence challenges, combined with blurry **time perception**, make it easy to lose track of time and relationships.

ALL MANUAL

- For ADHDers, **executive functions** like planning, organizing, prioritizing, and focusing **are not automatic.**
- These tasks must always be done **manually**, requiring conscious effort and draining **energy** throughout the day.
- The school system rarely provides **curiosity, stimulation, or interest**, making it especially challenging for ADHDers to thrive.

PARALYZING

Many things can paralyze ADHDers and autistic people:

- **Anxiety:** "What if it doesn't work? What if I fail anyway?"
- **Overwhelm:** Too many steps at once, like a computer freezing.

- **Not knowing where to start:** All the steps hit at once, and they can't identify the first one.
- **When things aren't 'as usual':** If a task doesn't follow its usual "script," it feels like a brand-new task.
- **Waiting paralysis:** Distorted time perception makes it impossible to start another task while waiting for something planned.
- **Inner dialogue:** A harsh inner monologue tells them, "It's not worth trying—you'll fail anyway."

- Paralysis isn't just "difficult"—it's often **impossible** to move or act, even when you're screaming at yourself to do so.
- Overcoming paralysis isn't about **effort**, because effort doesn't address the underlying problem.
- The mean **inner monologue**—a mix of voices from parents, teachers, and society—can make paralysis worse.
- Parents of ADHD kids can help by **avoiding harsh criticism** and offering **understanding and support.**
- For adults, starting your healing journey means understanding yourself, your brain, and the systems that shaped your experience.

WHY WE DON'T FINISH TASKS

- ADHDers may not finish tasks the **traditional way** (from start to finish in one go).
- They often complete projects **later** or by switching between tasks to keep the **dopamine high.**
- Factors like **lack of dopamine,** the **fear of what comes next,** and **low expectations from others** can make it harder to finish.
- ADHDers **can finish things**—just in their own way and on their own timeline.

SO, WHAT IS ADHD?

- **ADHD is a neurotype, not a disorder.** Neurotypes are ways the brain processes information, and ADHD, autism, and neurotypical are all valid neurotypes.
- ADHD behaviors are normal for ADHD brains—just like running after sheep is normal for a border collie but not for a chihuahua.
- Science is beginning to shift its perspective, recognizing ADHD as different, not broken.
- ADHD is about **differences in executive functions** and **variability in attention**, not a deficit. The name "ADHD" is misleading, and many have proposed alternatives like **DAVE** to better capture its nature.
- There's no such thing as **ADD** anymore, it's all considered **ADHD.**
- ADHD can involve **physical and mental hyperactivity** or just **mental hyperactivity.**
- **Cognitive hyperactivity** feels like having 50 browser tabs open at once, with your mind running nonstop.
- Inattentive ADHD is often **misunderstood and underdiagnosed** because it looks calm on the outside, but inside, it's chaotic.

THE POSITIVE SIDE OF ADHD

ADHD isn't just about struggles—it comes with some **amazing strengths.**

- ADHDers are **super curious,** always exploring and learning new things.

- They bring **unique problem-solving skills,** finding creative solutions that others might miss.
- Their **enthusiasm and passion** are infectious, inspiring those around them to get excited too.

With the right opportunities, people with ADHD can turn their **unique perspectives and energy** into powerful tools that allow them to **thrive and succeed** in all areas of life.

A WORD ABOUT AUTISM

- ADHD and autism brains approach tasks differently because of their unique **executive functioning challenges.**
- **ADHD struggles** with impulsivity, task initiation, and time management, while **autism struggles** with task-switching, cognitive flexibility, and sensory overload.
- Neurotypical tools don't always work—ADHD needs **dopamine-driven strategies** to get started, while autism benefits from **clear routines and predictable steps.**
- Embrace the strengths of each neurotype by working **with their operating system, not against it.**

THE CAPITALISM INFLUENCE

FROM THE EARLY AGE

Grades don't define intelligence, and memorizing facts isn't the same as being smart. **True intelligence** is about critical thinking, reasoning, and making connections. ADHDers and autistic people are often highly intelligent but need engaging, stimulating subjects to thrive—something that grades rarely reflect.

The education system values **memorization, routines,** and **sitting still,** which don't align with how ADHD brains are wired. This can make it easy to feel like you're not smart, but nothing could be further from the truth.

ADHDers are incredibly **creative**, with an unmatched ability to **think outside the box** and spot **connections others might miss.** They excel in ways that don't fit the school mold, like solving problems on the spot or diving deep into subjects they love. Unfortunately, these strengths often go **unrecognized** because traditional classrooms aren't designed to showcase them.

Intelligence isn't about grades, it's about **how you create, think,** and **approach the world.** If school has ever made you feel less than, remember: the system wasn't built to measure your kind of brilliance. Your **creativity, passion,** and unique perspective will thrive where traditional metrics fall short.

Comparing yourself to others, especially when you have ADHD, is often unfair and unproductive. Focus on **your growth**, appreciate the unique strengths you bring to the table, and remember that **everyone's path is different.** What works for them might not work for you, and that's okay. **You're doing your best, and that matters.**

From kindergarten, we're trained to compare ourselves to others based on grades, equating success with intelligence. But the **one-size-fits-all school system** doesn't suit everyone, especially ADHDers. Intelligence isn't about memorizing facts—it's about **creativity** and **critical thinking.** This emphasis on grades mirrors the workplace's focus on productivity, leading to **external validation** becoming a measure of self-worth.

The system wasn't built for ADHD brains, but you can create one that celebrates your strengths instead of trying to fit into a mold that doesn'

THE CAPITALIST SOCIETY

Society often bases our worth on how much money we make. Prestigious jobs bring respect, while not working leads to judgment. But more people are starting to realize how toxic this mindset is, shifting their focus to enjoying life and doing meaningful work. For ADHDers, capitalism's emphasis on productivity and rigid systems doesn't highlight their unique strengths, but that doesn't make them less valuable. Your worth isn't tied to your output—**it's tied to who you are.**

When we introduce ourselves, we often start with our jobs, making them a big part of our identity. While loving your work is great, your job is just **one part** of who you are. You're also a parent, a geek, a sportsman, an artist, and much more. Defining yourself by your job can be toxic, tying your worth to work achievements and leading to burnout. **Remember, you are more than just a worker or a student.**

We live in a performance-driven society that ties our worth to how much we can achieve. This pressure starts in childhood, teaching us to value grades and productivity over creativity, self-awareness, and personal growth. Teenagers, especially, face immense stress, leading to anxiety and low self-esteem. For ADHDers, this system is even more harmful because it forces them to adapt in ways that go against their nature. We need to redefine success to focus on **good deeds, helpfulness,** and **self-discovery**, not just academic or work achievements.

Parents play a big role in the pressure kids feel to succeed. Good grades are often met with pride and approval, while bad grades bring reprimands. For ADHDers, this can be especially tough since many parents still view academic struggles as a lack of effort rather than a reflection of how their child's brain works. Even without direct criticism, children pick up on subtle cues from their parents, conditioning themselves to strive for success to earn love and approval. The goal is for parents to become informed, empathetic, and the safest source of support for their kids.

As kids, we seek validation from our parents, often pushing ourselves to meet their expectations. But if we grow up constantly chasing approval from parents who are never satisfied, it can destroy our self-esteem and lead to anxiety. **The only approval you need is your own.** Focus on making **yourself proud**, on your terms, not theirs.

Your "best" changes depending on your energy, mood, stress, and circumstances. Struggling on a test or in any situation doesn't mean you didn't try hard enough, it means that was your best at that moment. Don't dwell on regret; instead, reflect on how you can adjust next time. Remember, your best today might not be your best tomorrow, and that's completely okay.

LAZINESS

Calling ADHDers "lazy" is common but completely ignores the bigger picture. Laziness is often a label capitalism uses to shame people for not working, tying their worth to productivity. This label shifts blame for poverty and unemployment onto individuals instead of addressing systemic issues like inequality. But laziness isn't real, it's just a judgment made without understanding the reasons behind someone's inaction, whether it's ADHD paralysis, exhaustion, or lack of motivation. Let's stop judging and start asking what's really going on.

An excuse is just a reason someone else doesn't think is valid. When people say, **"Don't use ADHD as an excuse,"** they're dismissing the valid reasons behind your ADHD traits. But your ADHD is a valid reason for your behavior. Also, "I don't want to" is a valid reason for not doing something, and it's different from "I don't feel like it," which means you'd rather do something else. Knowing the difference is important.

AGAINST OUR NATURE

"Society" refers to the shared values, rules, and beliefs we live by, but these aren't universal. In Canada, for example, professional success is highly valued, but this isn't true everywhere. Some countries, like Japan, overemphasize work, while others, like Holland, prioritize work-life balance. Recognizing that our way of life isn't the only "normal" lets us question what truly matters, understand our own needs, and live in a way that feels more natural and fulfilling, even within the constraints of an imperfect system.

Humans are like different dog breeds, we're all the same species, but our "wiring" is different. ADHDers and autistic people are wired differently from neurotypicals, just like a husky is wired differently from a bulldog. Forcing people with ADHD to function in a neurotypical society is like keeping a husky in a Florida apartment without exercise, it's unnatural, frustrating, and damaging. To thrive, we need environments that match our needs, just like dogs need environments suited to their instincts.

The North American school system isn't designed for ADHD brains. It expects everyone to sit still, follow strict schedules, and focus on repetitive tasks—all things that ADHDers struggle with. ADHD minds thrive on creativity, movement, and variety, but the current system often makes these students feel like they're falling behind or not smart enough. The problem isn't you—it's the system not recognizing your strengths.

The pressure to finish school fast, get a "good job," or make "6 figures" is an illusion. These ideas aren't universal truths—they're societal norms we've been taught. Different cultures prioritize different things, proving there's no one "right" way to live. Just like outdated rules about smoking or baby care, what seems normal now might not actually be good for us. Questioning these norms helps us live more authentically, even if change feels uncomfortable at first.

We're spending loads on mental health services but ignoring the root cause: the outdated norms and rules that stress people out. Living by these old values can hurt self-esteem, create constant stress, and fail to account for diversity, like different neurotypes. To truly support mental health, we need to question these norms and push for change that prioritizes well-being. Even if we can't change society overnight, recognizing the problem is the first step toward progress.

BEING A STUDENT WITH ADHD

THE SCHOOL SYSTEM

Homework mirrors unpaid overtime, and schools are more about creating workers than nurturing creativity. The rigid, standardized system works for neurotypical students but clashes with ADHD brains, which thrive on freedom, curiosity, and variety.

Most study tips and school strategies are designed for neurotypical learners, leaving ADHD students feeling like they're the problem when the real issue is the system itself. Undiagnosed ADHD students often struggle the most, blaming themselves for their difficulties.

The school system isn't changing anytime soon, but understanding that ADHD students *aren't the problem* is the first step toward supporting them in a system that wasn't built for their strengths.

THE PRIVILEGE OF DIAGNOSIS

Even if you believe in ADHD, most people can't afford a diagnosis, and free assessments are extremely rare. Schools often insist on having a diagnosis to offer accommodations, but this punishes struggling students who can't get one. Struggling should be enough to get help—whether there's a diagnosis or not. Accommodations shouldn't be gatekept behind an expensive process. Students deserve support based on their needs, not their access to healthcare.

THE ROLE OF TEACHERS

Teachers do more than teach, they're crucial to creating inclusive learning environments. By checking in with students individually and adapting their methods, they can support different learning styles. Celebrating neurodiversity makes the classroom stronger: students with ADHD might excel in creativity and problem-solving, while autistic students might shine in detailed work. When teachers focus on these strengths, they help students grow and enrich the learning experience for everyone.

UNDERSTANDING STRESS

Stress is your brain's natural reaction to anything it sees as a threat. Four key triggers are:

1. **Poor Control**: Feeling powerless over a situation.
2. **Unpredictability**: Not knowing what's coming next.
3. **Novelty**: Facing new or unfamiliar experiences.
4. **Threat to Ego**: Situations that challenge your self-image or confidence.

Understanding these stress factors can help you identify your triggers and take steps to manage them effectively.

Stress activates your body's **survival mode**, releasing adrenaline to make you stronger, faster, and more alert. Your heart pumps harder to send more blood and oxygen to your muscles, preparing you for action. At the same time, digestion slows, and your brain pauses memory and deep thinking to focus on immediate survival. While stress is great for quick reactions, staying in this state for too long can take a serious toll on your health.

Your brain reacts to tests like they're life-or-death situations because it's wired to protect you from danger. Society makes tests feel super important for your future and self-worth, so your brain treats them as major threats. This stress response is normal, but it's also why you might feel overwhelmed or blank out—it's just your brain doing what it's designed to do.

Stress happens, but you have tools to manage it. Tensing and relaxing your body tricks your brain into calming down. Moving your body releases built-up tension. Backup plans ease the stress of unpredictability, and music can distract your mind enough to break the stress cycle. Focus on what you can control—like your actions and mindset—rather than what's out of your hands. Small steps can make a big difference in reducing stress!

DOING YOUR BEST

"Doing your best" means doing the best you can in the moment, not breaking your all-time record every time. Think of it like running a 5K—some days you'll beat your personal best, and some days you won't, but the goal is to slowly improve your average.

If life throws challenges your way—poor sleep, stress, or bad luck—it's okay if your best isn't as good as yesterday. Improvement is about progress, not perfection. Remember, you're doing great! Keep going.

IMPACTS OF ADHD AND AUTISM ON STUDIES AND LEARNING

Being a neurodivergent student with ADHD can feel like juggling flaming swords while riding a unicycle. Challenges like staying focused, managing time, and dealing with memory hiccups are part of the daily struggle.

- **Memory isn't about effort**—your brain decides what to forget, not you.
- **Boredom is the enemy**—without enough stimulation, focus evaporates.
- School isn't built for the ADHD brain, but that doesn't mean you can't find ways to thrive.

Whether it's using tools to stay organized (and remembering to check them!) or finding ways to make learning more exciting, the key is working *with* your brain—not against it.

Now for autistic people

- **Clear instructions** are essential—they need to know exactly what's expected to avoid unnecessary stress.
- **Communication challenges** arise when literal interpretations clash with implied meanings, so be precise.
- **Sensory sensitivities** (buzzing lights, itchy tags, loud noises) can make it hard to focus—it's not just a preference, it's a real struggle.
- **Routine and structure** help them thrive; unexpected changes can cause anxiety and throw off their focus.

HOW EDUCATORS CAN SUPPORT NEURODIVERSITY IN SCHOOL

CREATING A SAFE SPACE

1. **Zero tolerance isn't enough**: Bullying persists without active intervention and a culture of inclusion.
2. **Reinforce good behavior**: Celebrate kindness and reward positive actions to encourage a supportive environment.
3. **Support both victims and bullies**: Address the root causes of bullying while helping victims heal and thrive.
4. **Involve professionals if needed**: School counselors or psychologists can offer deeper support to both sides.

True safety isn't about punishment—it's about teaching kindness, empathy, and respect. By focusing on the positive and addressing issues compassionately, schools can create spaces where every student feels valued and secure.

IN THE CLASSROOM

1. **Reframe ADHD behaviors** as part of the learning process, not disruptions.
2. **Celebrate strengths** to boost confidence and break the "not good enough" mindset.
3. Create a **safe, supportive environment** where mistakes are learning opportunities and communication is encouraged.
4. Make learning accessible with **movement breaks**, flexible seating, clear instructions, and alternative assessments.
5. Foster a culture of **empathy and inclusivity**, preparing students to value differences in school and beyond.

With understanding, patience, and small changes, teachers can help ADHD students—and all students—thrive in a supportive, inclusive classroom.

SOME TIPS FOR AUTISTIC STUDENTS

1. **Use clear, literal language** and avoid ambiguous phrases. If they're confused, rephrase with patience, don't dismiss their concerns.
2. **Be patient with communication**: Allow extra time to process and respond; accept alternative forms of communication.
3. **Understand shutdowns and meltdowns**: These are involuntary. Speak to parents to learn how to support the student best.

    ○   **Shutdowns**: The student may freeze and become unresponsive.
    ○   **Meltdowns**: The student may scream or hit out of distress.

4. **Minimize unexpected changes**: Give advance notice for schedule changes or tests, and explain them clearly.

These strategies—paired with compassion and understanding—create a classroom where autistic students feel safe, supported, and able to thrive.

HUMAN RESOURCES TO HELP

- **Academic Advisors**: More than class schedulers, they help balance your workload, create routines, and connect you with clubs or activities that match your interests. They're your personal guide for school *and* life.
- **Counselors**: High school or college can feel overwhelming, but counselors are there to support you through stress, homesickness, and big life changes. They make sure you don't just survive, but thrive.
- **Tutors**: Stuck on a tricky subject? Tutors break down material in a way that makes sense, teach you study habits, and boost your confidence. They're your personal guide to staying on track and succeeding in school.

Finding support from advisors, counselors, and tutors can make school less stressful and help you feel more confident, organized, and capable.

LEARNING AND STUDIES

BASIC NEEDS

1. **Food and Water**: Your brain needs good fuel to focus, stay awake, and remember things. Healthy food and clean water keep you sharp.

2. **Shelter**: A safe, stable place to live gives you the peace of mind to concentrate on school.

3. **Sleep**: Rest recharges your brain, improving focus, energy, and stress management.

4. **Clothing**: Wearing weather-appropriate clothes keeps you comfortable and less distracted.

5. **Safety**: Feeling safe at home, school, and in your community lets you focus and stay motivated.

6. **Health**: Physical health gives you the energy and stamina to tackle schoolwork.

7. **Financial Stability**: Less stress about money means better access to resources and fewer distractions.

8. **Love and Support**: Feeling cared for by family or friends builds confidence, reduces stress, and keeps you motivated.

If these needs aren't fully met, it's normal to struggle with learning. Focus on what you *can* fix, and be kind to yourself, you're doing your best, and that's what really counts.

COGNITIVE BIASES

1. **Confirmation Bias**: You only notice what supports your beliefs and ignore the rest. If you think you're bad at something, you focus on failures and dismiss successes.

2. **Fixed Mindset**: Believing your abilities can't change makes you avoid challenges and fear failure instead of seeing them as opportunities to grow.

3. **Self-Serving Bias**: Taking credit for successes but blaming failures on outside factors. It stops you from learning and improving.

4. **Sunk Cost Fallacy**: Sticking with something that isn't working because you've already invested time or energy. Sometimes it's better to move on.

5. **Spotlight Effect**: Thinking everyone's paying attention to you when, really, they're focused on themselves. Don't let this stop you from trying.

6. **Overconfidence Bias**: Assuming you're more prepared than you are, which can lead to underpreparation and disappointment.

7. **Availability Heuristic**: Overestimating something's likelihood because it's fresh in your mind. One failure doesn't mean it will happen again.

8. **Bandwagon Effect**: Doing something because "everyone else is," even if it's not right for you. Stick to your own values and goals.

9. **Anchoring Bias**: Relying too much on the first information you hear. Don't let first impressions dictate your experience.

10. **Negativity Bias**: Focusing more on negative experiences than positive ones. Celebrate your wins and remember your strengths.

11. **False Consensus Effect**: Believing everyone feels or thinks the same as you. You're not alone—most people face struggles, even if they don't show it.

Understanding these biases helps you recognize when they're holding you back and make better, more balanced decisions. By challenging these patterns, you can boost your confidence, motivation, and ability to grow!

- Saying yes to something small makes it easier to say yes to bigger things later. For ADHD students, this can mean skipping one small task leads to skipping more and more.
- **How it holds you back**: Small exceptions snowball into procrastination, eventually derailing your entire plan.
- **How to avoid it**:

1. Catch yourself when you're tempted to skip.

2. Commit to small wins (do 5 minutes instead of skipping entirely).
3. Keep the big picture in mind: small steps matter.
4. Set rules to hold yourself accountable.
5. Track your progress to stay motivated.

MOTIVATION AND PROCRASTINATION

- **Motivation** is the **reason** behind what you do, it's your destination.
- **Energy** or interest is like the fuel that moves you along the path.
- If you lack motivation, it often means you haven't found your **"why"** yet.
- Without knowing your purpose, it's hard to find the energy to keep going.

Find your "why," refuel your energy, and take small steps toward your destination. The clearer your purpose, the easier it is to stay driven!

- **What it is**: Procrastination is delaying tasks, often to dodge frustration, boredom, or fear of failure.
- **Why it happens**: ADHD brains crave dopamine, so boring or overwhelming tasks feel harder to stick with.
- **Active procrastination**: Even when you avoid one task, you can still get productive things done—like cleaning or organizing.
- **How to handle it**: Recognize what's holding you back, take small steps, and use active procrastination to build momentum.

Procrastination doesn't have to derail you—understand what's behind it, and use it to your advantage. Balance and self-awareness are key!

HOW TO LEARN AND STUDY

ACTIVE LEARNING

Being taught is passive: it's when someone gives you information. **Learning** is active: it's when you take that information, process it, and make it your own. Schools often focus on teaching, but real learning happens when you practice and actively engage with what you're taught. For ADHD brains, finding ways to actively learn is key to making the information stick.

- **Active learning** means getting involved, don't just sit back and hope the info sticks.
- **Patterns and connections** make learning easier, not random memorization.
- Use the **"See one, do one, teach one"** method: Watch, try, and teach to solidify your understanding.
- **Self-discipline** helps move info from short-term to long-term memory.
-
- **Avoid memorization**: Focus on understanding, not cramming facts.
- **Learn from mistakes**: They're opportunities to grow, not failures. Use them to improve your approach and deepen your knowledge.
- **Find your system**: Study how it works for you—whether it's silence, noise, one task at a time, or switching between tasks.

Make learning your own. Engage with it, embrace mistakes, and discover what works best for you!

GETTING IN ACTION

Getting started is hard, but it's a skill you can build. Don't wait for the "perfect" choice. **Pick something and start,** even if it's not the right fit, switching is faster than staying stuck in indecision. The key is to move forward!

Turn active procrastination into a tool. Completing small tasks builds momentum and confidence, making it easier to tackle the big task. Celebrate the small victories, and you'll find the big one feels far less overwhelming.

Don't aim for perfect—just doing **something** is better than doing nothing. Finishing, even imperfectly, is a win. Celebrate small victories, focus on progress over perfection, and remember that starting imperfectly is still starting.

Stuck? Countdown from 5 to 0, then take the first step, like standing up or opening your book. It's a simple brain hack to stop overthinking and start moving. Once you're in motion, it's easier to keep going.

Your **green zone** is when you're at peak energy, use it for important tasks. Save lighter work for your **yellow zone** and rest during your **red zone**. Working with your natural energy flow makes your day more productive and less stressful.

For ADHD, tasks become easier if they're **Interesting, New, Challenging, or Urgent**. Use these criteria to tweak tasks: gamify them, add deadlines, or create mini-goals. It's about working with how your brain naturally works, not forcing it.

Use a **5-minute timer** or two songs to tackle a task without pressure to finish. The goal is to start and make progress. Quick sprints like this break the barrier of starting and can lead to surprising productivity by the end of the day!

Don't wait for motivation. Take **action first**, even if it's small. Action triggers dopamine, which makes you feel good and motivates you to do more. Celebrate your victories (big or small), and keep the cycle going. Motivation comes after action, not before.

Being hard on yourself doesn't work, so try kindness instead. Your brain works differently, and that's not your fault. Treat yourself like you'd treat a friend: with patience, compassion, and respect. You're doing your best, and that's enough.

For overwhelming tasks, **break them into tiny, specific steps** like "wash one plate" or "write one sentence." Focus on one step at a time, and if the full list feels like too much, hide it. Work backward to create a roadmap if needed. Small steps add up to big accomplishments, and every tiny win fuels your momentum.

Trick your brain into productivity by linking cues, like music, clothes, or smells, to specific tasks. These signals help your brain switch into the right mode automatically, making starting tasks easier without relying on willpower.

Feeling stuck? Ask someone you trust to be your **body double**. Their presence can motivate you, ease the stress, and help you get started. Needing help isn't failure, it's just the nudge you need to push forward.

Stuck starting a project? Immerse yourself in the topic, watch, read, and listen to build excitement. Let the hype push you into action, but make sure the process inspires confidence, not self-doubt!

Feeling low energy? Use online resources like videos, podcasts, and articles to gather knowledge and inspiration without leaving your couch. Even small steps can lead to big progress!

STAYING IN ACTION

Start with a small, easy task like picking up one shirt or reading one line of your textbook. The "meh, might as well" principle keeps you going step by step, turning tiny actions into real progress without feeling overwhelmed, because once you've done something small, meh, might as well do the next step!

Switch up your workspace or tools to add novelty and break the monotony. A new environment or setup can refresh your focus and make it easier to dive into your tasks.

The Pomodoro Method helps you stay focused with short work sessions (10-60 minutes) followed by 5-minute breaks. After four cycles, take a 20-minute break. It reduces overwhelm, keeps distractions in check, and turns productivity into a game!

Use rewards to keep yourself motivated. Break tasks into small steps, set rewards for each win, and choose things you love. Mix up your rewards to keep things exciting, and watch as even boring tasks feel more doable!

ADHD brains need stimulation to focus. Use music, background noise, or multitasking to stay engaged. Take quick, fun breaks and adjust your environment to suit your needs. It's all about finding what works for you to keep tasks interesting and manageable!

If it works, it's a good system! Take time to learn your unique style, mix and match strategies, and experiment to find the perfect approach.

Tailor everything to fit your needs, there's no wrong way if it helps you succeed!

ORGANIZATION AND PLANNING

Feeling stuck? Use a to-do list to map out your tasks and break them into smaller, manageable steps. Prioritize important and urgent tasks with tools like the Eisenhower Matrix. Build the habit of checking your list with creative tools like journals, apps, or sticky notes. It'll help you stay on track and feel accomplished!

ADHD brains thrive with **visual reminders**. Use sticky notes or a whiteboard to keep important tasks front and center. Refresh reminders regularly to keep them noticeable, and don't forget to make them colorful and fun!

Alarms and timers are ADHD-friendly tools for managing time. Use alarms to structure your day and timers for short focus bursts (like the Pomodoro method). Avoid snoozing by using energizing sounds, placing alarms out of reach, and moving immediately when they ring. They work best when used consistently!

Your brain only remembers what it actually pays attention to. If you can't recall where you put something, it's not that you forgot; your brain might not have registered it at all. This is common with ADHD, so be patient with yourself.

www.ingramcontent.com/pod-product-compliance
Lightning Source LLC
Chambersburg PA
CBHW071958260326
41914CB00004B/845